easy to make!
Everyday Vegetarian

D0178935

H46 320 286 3

Good Housekeeping

easy to make!
Everyday
Vegetarian

COLLINS & BROWN

This editon published in Great Britian in 2012
by Collins & Brown
10 Southcombe Street
London W14 0RA

An imprint of Anova Books Company Ltd

Copyright © The National Magazine Company Limited
and Collins & Brown 2012

All rights reserved. No part of this publication may be
reproduced, stored in a retrieval system, or transmitted in any
form or by any means, electronic, mechanical, photocopying,
recording or otherwise, without the prior written consent of the
copyright holder.

The expression Good Housekeeping as used in the title
of the book is the trademark of the National Magazine Company
and The Hearst Corporation, registered in the United Kingdom
and USA, and other principal countries of the world, and is the
absolute property of The National Magazine Company and The
Hearst Corporation. The use of this trademark other than with
the express permission of The National Magazine Company or
The Hearst Corporation is strictly prohibited.

The Good Housekeeping website is
www.goodhousekeeping.co.uk

10 9 8 7 6 5 4 3 2 1

ISBN 978-1-90844-911-5

A catalogue record for this book is available from the British
Library.

Reproduced by Dot Gradations Ltd
Printed and bound by Times Printing, Malaysia

This book can be ordered direct from the publisher at
www.anovabooks.com

NOTES

- Both metric and imperial measures are given for the recipes. Follow either set of measures, not a mixture of both, as they are not interchangeable.
- All spoon measures are level.
  1 tsp = 5ml spoon; 1 tbsp = 15ml spoon.
- Ovens and grills must be preheated to the specified temperature.
- Use sea salt and freshly ground black pepper unless otherwise suggested.
- Fresh herbs should be used unless dried herbs are specified in a recipe.
- Medium eggs should be used except where otherwise specified. Free-range eggs are recommended.
- Note that certain recipes, including mayonnaise, lemon curd and some cold desserts, contain raw or lightly cooked eggs. The young, elderly, pregnant women and anyone with an immune-deficiency disease should avoid these, because of the slight risk of salmonella.
- Calorie, fat and carbohydrate counts per serving are provided for the recipes.

Picture Credits
Photographers: Neil Barclay (pages 36 and 52); Martin Brigdale
(pages 39 and 61); Nicki Dowey (pages 33, 35, 37, 41, 42, 44, 47,
50, 51, 53, 55, 56, 58, 70, 71, 74, 75, 82, 89, 92, 95, 96, 99, 100,
101, 106, 107, 108, 111, 113, 118, 119, 120, 121, 122, 124, 125
and 126); Will Heap (page 38); Craig Robertson (Basics
photography and pages 34, 40, 45, 57, 60, 62, 63, 69, 72, 73, 76,
77, 79, 80, 81, 87, 90, 91, 93, 104, 109, 110 and 112); Lucinda
Symons (pages 65, 88, 97 and 117)
Stylists: Wei Tang, Helen Trent and Fanny Ward
Home Economists: Joanna Farrow, Emma Jane Frost, Teresa
Goldfinch, Alice Hart, Lucy McKelvie, Kim Morphew and Mari
Mererid Williams

Contents

Foreword

Cooking, for me, is one of life's great pleasures. Not only is it necessary to fuel your body, but it exercises creativity, skill, social bonding and patience. The science behind the cooking also fascinates me, and learning how yeast works, or grasping why certain flavours marry quite so well is (in my mind) to become a good cook.

I've often encountered people who claim not to be able to cook – they're just not interested or say they simply don't have time. My sister won't mind me saying that she was one of those who sat firmly in the camp of disinterested domestic goddess. But things change, and she realized that my mother (an excellent cook) wouldn't always be on hand to prepare steaming home-cooked meals, and that she actually wanted to be able to whip up good food for her own family one day. All it took was some good cookbooks (naturally, Good Housekeeping was present and accounted for) and some enthusiasm, and sure enough, she is now a kitchen wizard, creating such confections that baffle even me.

I've been lucky enough to have a love for all things culinary for as long as I can remember. Baking rock-like chocolate cakes and misshapen biscuits was a rite of passage that I cherish. I made my mistakes young, so have lost the fear of cookery mishaps. I think it's these mishaps that scare people, but when you realize that a mistake made once will seldom be repeated, your domination of the kitchen can start.

This Good Housekeeping Easy to Make! collection is filled with tantalizing recipes that have been triple tested (at least!) in our dedicated test kitchens. They have been developed to be easily achievable, delicious and guaranteed to work – taking the element of chance out of cookery.

I hope you enjoy this collection and that it inspires you to get cooking.

Meike.

Meike Beck
Cookery Editor
Good Housekeeping

0

The Basics

Nutrition

Whether you are already a commited vegetarian, are thinking of giving up meat and fish altogether, or simply fancy having one or two meat-free days a week, you will want to ensure that you and your family are getting a good balanced diet.

A vegetarian diet

A vegetarian diet is one that excludes meat, poultry and fish. Many vegetarians also avoid other animal products such as gelatine, animal fats such as lard and suet, and animal rennet in non-vegetarian cheeses. However, the majority of vegetarians do eat dairy produce, including milk, cheese and free-range eggs. Provided that a vegetarian diet includes a good range of cereals and grains, pulses, nuts and seeds, fruit and vegetables, dairy and/or soya products, it is unlikely to be nutritionally deficient, but variety is important to ensure a good intake of protein.

A vegan diet

Vegans follow a more restrictive diet, which excludes, in addition to meat, poultry and fish, all dairy products, eggs, and even foods such as honey, because it is produced by bees. A vegan diet can be deficient in vitamin B12, which is only present in animal and dairy foods. To make up for this, fortified breakfast cereals, yeast extract and/or soya milk should be consumed. Soya products are a particularly valuable source of protein, energy, vitamin B12, vitamin D, calcium, minerals and beneficial omega-3 fatty acids.

Balancing a vegetarian or vegan diet

Many people assume that a vegetarian's diet is automatically healthier than that of a carnivore. This isn't always the case – there are good and bad vegetarian diets. It is not enough simply to stop eating meat: the nutrients that would normally be obtained from meat must be replaced. It's quite common for vegetarians to rely too heavily on dairy products such as cheese and eggs, which can be high in saturated fats and calories. Such a limited diet is not only unhealthy but will also eventually become boring. As with any diet, variety is important. It is useful to have a basic understanding of nutrition and the importance of certain foods – if only to convince meat-eaters that a vegetarian diet can be healthy.

Protein

Contrary to popular belief, there are lots of good vegetable sources of protein, such as beans, grains, nuts, soya products and Quorn, as well as eggs, cheese, milk and yogurt. Protein is made up of smaller units called amino acids. These are needed for the manufacture and repair of body cells, so they are very important. The body can manufacture some amino acids itself, but others, known as the essential amino acids, must come from food. Animal protein contains almost all of these and is therefore known as a 'complete' protein.

With the exception of soya products, vegetable proteins are lacking or low in one or more amino acid. However, by eating certain foods together at the same meal, any deficiency is overcome. This isn't as complicated as it sounds and usually happens automatically when menu planning. For example, pulses and nuts should be eaten with cereals or dairy products – such as muesli with yogurt or milk, chilli beans with rice, nut roast made with breadcrumbs, peanut butter on toast, dhal with raita, or nut burgers with a bap.

Vitamins

Vitamins are vital for proper body functioning. They can be divided into two categories – fat soluble and water soluble. Fat-soluble vitamins A, D, E and K are found mostly in foods that contain fat. They are stored in the body by the liver. The water-soluble vitamins C and B-complex dissolve in water and cannot be stored by the body, so a regular supply is important.
A varied diet should supply all the vitamins our bodies need. Vegetarians and vegans should ensure that their intake of vitamins B12 and D is sufficient, although a deficiency of either is unlikely.

Make the most of vitamins

For maximum vitamin retention, buy fruit and vegetables in peak condition, preferably from a shop with a fast turnover of stock. Eat them as soon as possible. Wilted or old vegetables have a lower vitamin content than fresh.
Store vegetables in a cool, dark place: light is destructive to vitamins, especially vitamins B and C. Don't leave bottles of milk on the doorstep: vitamin B2 (riboflavin) is destroyed when exposed to ultraviolet light.
Steam or boil vegetables until just tender, using the minimum amount of water.
Don't add soda to cooking water. Once vegetables have been cooked and drained, use the water for stocks, gravies and soups.
Don't prepare vegetables hours in advance and leave them soaking in water. Leave the skin on whenever you can.
Eat plenty of raw vegetables and fruit.
Vitamin loss continues after cooking, particularly when warm foods are left waiting around, so eat soon after cooking.

Minerals

Minerals cannot be manufactured by the body and must be obtained from food. At present, 15 minerals have been identified as being essential to health and others are under investigation. Most people obtain enough minerals provided that a good variety of foods is eaten. Iron, calcium and zinc are the three minerals most often discussed in relation to a vegetarian diet.

Sources of protein

Most vegetarians needn't worry about getting enough protein: this nutrient is found in a wide variety of foods including pulses, tofu and other soya bean products, Quorn, eggs, cheese, and sprouted beans and seeds.

Meat substitutes

Pulses

The term 'pulse' is used to describe all the various beans, peas and lentils. Pulses are highly nutritious, especially when eaten with grains such as couscous, pasta, rice or bread. Dried pulses should be stored in airtight containers in a cool, dry cupboard. They keep well, but after about six months their skins start to toughen and they take progressively longer to cook. Most pulses must be soaked prior to cooking. Canned pulses are a convenient, quick alternative to having to soak and cook dried ones, and most supermarkets stock a wide range. A 400g can (drained weight about 235g) is roughly equivalent to 100g (3½oz) dried beans. Dried pulses double in weight after soaking.

Sprouted beans and seeds

These are rich in nutrients and lend a nutty taste and crunchy texture to salads and stir-fries. Fresh bean sprouts are available from most supermarkets. Many beans and seeds can be sprouted at home, though it is important to buy ones that are specifically produced for sprouting – from a health food shop or other reliable source. Mung beans, aduki beans, alfalfa seeds and fenugreek are all suitable.

Cheese

Some vegetarians prefer to avoid cheeses that have been produced by the traditional method, because this uses animal-derived rennet. Most supermarkets and cheese shops now stock an excellent range of vegetarian cheeses, produced using vegetarian rennet that comes from plants such as thistle and mallow, which contain enzymes capable of curdling milk.

Tofu

Also known as bean curd, tofu is made from ground soya beans in a process akin to cheese-making. It is highly nutritious but virtually tasteless. However, it readily absorbs other flavours when marinated.

Tofu is sold as a chilled product and should be stored in the fridge. Once the packet is opened, the tofu should be kept immersed in a bowl of water in the fridge and eaten within four days.

Firm tofu is usually cut into chunks, then immersed in tasty marinades or dressings prior to grilling, stir-frying, deep-frying, adding to stews, or tossing raw into salads. It can also be chopped and made into burgers and nut roasts.

Smoked tofu has more flavour than unsmoked; it is used in the same way but doesn't need marinating.

Silken tofu is softer and creamier than firm tofu and is useful for making sauces and dressings.

Textured vegetable protein (TVP)

TVP forms the bulk of most ready-prepared vegetarian burgers, sausages and mince. It is made from a mixture of soya flour, flavourings and liquid, which is cooked, then extruded under pressure and cut into chunks or small pieces to resemble mince. It has a slightly chewy, meat-like texture. TVP can be included in stews, pies, curries and other dishes, rather as meat would be used by non-vegetarians.

Quorn

Quorn is a vegetarian product derived from a distant relative of the mushroom. Although it is not suitable for vegans because it contains egg albumen, Quorn is a good source of complete protein for vegetarians. Like tofu, Quorn has a bland flavour and benefits from being marinated before cooking. Find it in the chiller cabinet at the supermarket, and keep it in the fridge.

Asparagus

1 Cut or snap off the woody stem of each asparagus spear about 5cm (2in) from the stalk's end, or where the white and green sections meet. Or cut off the woody stem and peel the spear with a vegetable peeler or small, sharp knife.

Cook's Tips

To roast asparagus, drizzle with olive oil, a few spoonfuls of water and a little salt and roast in a preheated oven, 200°C (180°C fan oven) mark 6, for 12–15 minutes, depending on the thickness of the asparagus.
To cook in water, heat a large pan of salted water that will hold the asparagus in a single layer. Put in the spears and simmer for 5 minutes until tender, then drain.

Preparing vegetables

These frequently used vegetables can be quickly prepared to add flavour to savoury dishes: onions and shallots have a pungent taste that becomes milder when they are cooked, while tomatoes and peppers add depth and richness to a variety of dishes.

Mushrooms

Button, white, chestnut and flat mushrooms are all prepared in a similar way.

1 Wipe with a damp cloth or pastry brush to remove any dirt.

2 With button mushrooms, cut off the stalk flush with the base of the cap. For other mushrooms, cut a thin disc off the end of the stalk and discard. Chop or slice the mushrooms.

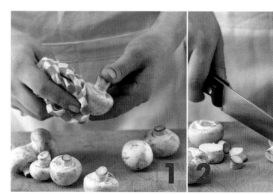

Fennel

1 Trim off the upper stems and the base of the bulbs. Remove the core with a small, sharp knife if it seems tough.

2 The outer leaves may be discoloured and can be scrubbed gently in cold water, or you can peel away the discoloured parts with a knife or a vegetable peeler. Slice the fennel or cut it into quarters, according to your recipe.

Leeks

As some leeks harbour a lot of grit and earth between their leaves, they need careful cleaning.

1 Cut off the root and any tough parts of the leek. Make a cut into the leaf end of the leek, about 7.5cm (3in) deep.

2 Hold under the cold tap while separating the cut halves to expose any grit. Wash well, then shake dry. Use the green tops for stock.

Seeding tomatoes

1 Halve the tomato through the core. Use a spoon or a small, sharp knife to remove the seeds and juice. Shake off the excess liquid.

2 Chop the tomato as required for your recipe and place in a colander for a minute or two, to drain off any excess liquid.

Peeling tomatoes

1 Fill a bowl or pan with boiling water. Using a slotted spoon, carefully add the tomato and leave for 15–30 seconds, then remove to a chopping board.

2 Use a small, sharp knife to cut out the core in a single cone-shaped piece. Discard the core.

3 Peel off the skin; it should come away easily, depending on ripeness.

  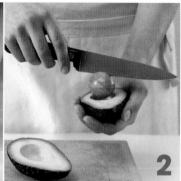 

Cutting tomatoes

1 Use a small, sharp knife to cut out the core in a single cone-shaped piece. Discard the core.

2 **Wedges** Halve the tomato and then cut into quarters or into three.

3 **Slices** Hold the tomato with the cored side on the chopping board for greater stability and use a serrated knife to cut into slices.

Tomato Sauce

To serve 4, you will need:
1 tbsp olive oil, 1 small onion, chopped, 1 carrot, grated, 1 celery stick, chopped, 1 garlic clove, crushed, ½ tbsp tomato purée, 2 x 400g cans plum tomatoes, 1 bay leaf, ½ tsp oregano, 2 tsp caster sugar.

1 Heat the oil in a pan. Add the onion, carrot and celery, then fry gently for 20 minutes until softened.

2 Add the garlic and tomato purée and fry for 1 minute. Stir in the tomatoes, add the bay leaf, oregano and sugar and simmer for 30 minutes until thickened.

Avocados

Prepare avocados just before serving, because their flesh discolours quickly once exposed to air.

1 Halve the avocado lengthways and twist the two halves apart. Tap the stone with a sharp knife, then twist to remove the stone.

2 Run a knife between the flesh and skin and pull the skin away. Slice the flesh.

Seeding peppers

The seeds and white pith of peppers taste bitter, so should be removed.

1 Cut off the top of the pepper, then cut away and discard the seeds and white pith.

2 Alternatively, cut the pepper in half vertically and snap out the white pithy core and seeds. Trim away the rest of the white membrane with a knife.

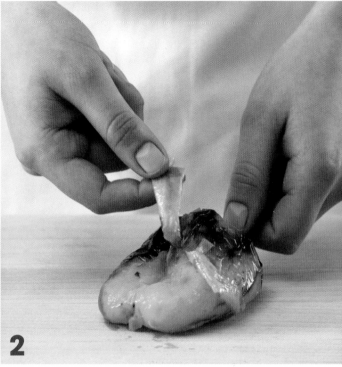

Chargrilling peppers

Charring imparts a smoky flavour and makes peppers easier to peel.

1 Hold the pepper, using tongs, over the gas flame on your hob (or under a preheated grill) until the skin blackens, turning until black all over.

2 Put in a bowl, cover and leave to cool (the steam will help to loosen the skin). Peel.

Spicy Red Pepper Dip

To serve 8, you will need:
3 large red peppers, about 450g (1lb) total weight, halved, 200g tub reduced-fat soft cheese, ½ tsp hot pepper sauce.

1 Preheat the grill. Chargrill the peppers as above, then peel and seed.

2 Put the flesh in a food processor or blender with the remaining ingredients. Purée until smooth. Cover and leave to chill for at least 2 hours to let the flavours develop. Taste and adjust the seasoning if necessary.

Pesto

To serve 4, you will need:
50g (2oz) fresh basil leaves, roughly torn, 1–2 garlic cloves, 25g (1oz) pinenuts, 6 tbsp extra virgin olive oil, 2 tbsp freshly grated Parmesan, lemon juice (optional), salt and ground black pepper.

1 Put the basil in a food processor with the garlic, pinenuts and 2 tbsp olive oil. Blend to a fairly smooth paste. Gradually add the remaining oil and season.

2 Transfer to a bowl and stir in the Parmesan. Add a squeeze of lemon juice if you like. Store in the refrigerator: cover with a thin layer of olive oil and seal tightly. It will keep for up to three days.

Shallots

1 Cut off the tip and trim off the ends of the root. Peel off the skin and any discoloured layers underneath.

2 Holding the shallot root-end down, use a small, sharp knife to make deep parallel slices almost down to the base, while keeping the slices attached to it.

3 **Slicing** Turn the shallot on its side and cut off slices from the base.

4 **Dicing** Make deep parallel slices at right angles to the first slices. Turn the shallot on its side and cut off the slices from the base. You should now have fine dice, but chop any larger pieces individually.

Onions

1 Cut off the tip and base of the onion. Peel away all the layers of papery skin and any discoloured layers underneath.

2 Put the onion, root-end down, on the chopping board and then, using a sharp knife, cut the onion in half from tip to base.

3 **Slicing** Put one half on the board, with the cut surface facing down, and slice across the onion.

4 **Chopping** Slice the halved onions, from the root end to the top, at regular intervals. Next, make 2–3 horizontal slices through the onion, then slice vertically across the width.

Carrots

1 Using a sharp knife, trim off the ends.

2 Using a vegetable peeler, peel off the skin in long strips.

Cutting aubergines

1 Trim the aubergine to remove the stalk and end.

2 **Slicing** Cut the aubergine into slices as thick as the pieces you will need for your recipe.

3 **Cutting and dicing** Stack the slices and cut across them to the appropriate size for fingers. Cut in the opposite direction for dice.

Stuffing aubergines

1 To hollow out an aubergine for stuffing, cut off the stalk and halve the aubergine lengthways.

2 Make deep incisions in the flesh, using a crisscross pattern, being careful not to pierce the skin.

3 Using a spoon, scoop out the flesh, leaving the skin intact, and use according to your recipe.

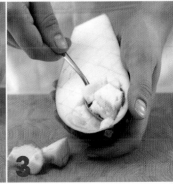

1

Using beans and lentils

Many dried beans and peas need to be soaked overnight before cooking. Lentils do not need soaking and are quicker to cook. Quicker still are canned beans: they are ready to use, but should be drained in a sieve and rinsed in cold water first.

Cooking beans

1 Pick through the beans to remove any grit or small stones. Put the beans in a bowl or pan and pour cold water over them to cover generously. Leave to soak for at least 8 hours, then drain. (If you are in a hurry, pour boiling water over the beans and leave them to cool in the water for 1–2 hours.)

2 Put the soaked beans in a large pan and add cold water to cover by at least 5cm (2in). Bring to the boil and boil rapidly for 10 minutes to destroy any toxins present in their skin.

3 Skim off the scum that rises to the top, turn down the heat and leave to simmer until the beans are soft inside (see cooking times below). They should be tender but not falling apart. Check periodically to make sure there's enough water to keep the beans well covered. Drain well. If using in a salad, allow to cool completely.

Cooking times

Times vary for different dried beans, peas and lentils. Older beans will take longer to cook, so use them within their 'best before' date.

Chickpeas	1–2 hours
Red kidney, cannellini, borlotti, butter beans and flageolet beans	1–3 hours
Red lentils	20 minutes
Green lentils	30–40 minutes

Cooking rice, grains and pasta

There are two main types of rice: long-grain and short-grain. Short-grain rice is used for dishes such as risotto, sushi and paella. Long-grain rice is generally used as an accompaniment or in salads. With any grain, the cooking time depends on how the grain has been processed. Cooked couscous, bulgur wheat and quinoa are all great in salads, as is pasta.

Preparing long-grain rice

Long-grain rice needs no special preparation, though basmati should be washed to remove excess starch.

1 Put in a bowl and cover with cold water. Stir until this becomes cloudy, then drain and repeat the washing process until the water is clear.

2 Soak the rice for 30 minutes, then drain before cooking.

Cooking long-grain rice

1 Measure the rice by volume and put it in a pan with a pinch of salt and twice the volume of boiling water (or boiling stock).

2 Bring to the boil. Turn the heat down to low, and set the timer for the time stated on the pack. It needs to end up al dente: tender, but with a hint of bite at the centre.

3 When the rice is cooked, fluff up the grains by gently tossing with a fork: this keeps the grains from sticking together. For using in salads, toss with a little salad dressing of your choice and leave to cool.

Perfect rice

• Use 50–75g (2–3oz) raw rice per person – or measure by volume 50–75ml (2–2½fl oz).
• If you often cook rice, you may want to invest in a special rice steamer. They are available in Asian supermarkets and some kitchen shops and give good, consistent results.

Couscous

Often mistaken for a grain, couscous is actually a type of pasta that originated in North Africa. It is perfect for making into salads or serving with stews and casseroles. The tiny pellets do not require cooking and can simply be soaked.

1 Measure the couscous in a jug and add 1½ times the volume of hot water or stock.

2 Cover the bowl and leave to soak for 5 minutes. Fluff up with a fork before serving.

3 If using for a salad, leave the couscous to cool completely before adding the other salad ingredients.

Bulgur wheat

A form of cracked wheat, bulgur has had some or all of the bran removed. It can be used in salads or served as an accompaniment. It is pre-boiled during manufacture and may be boiled, steamed or soaked.

Simmering Put the bulgur in a pan and cover with water by about 2.5cm (1in). Bring to the boil, then simmer for 10–15 minutes until just tender. Drain well.

Steaming Line a steamer with a clean teatowel, place the bulgur in the steamer and steam over boiling water for 20 minutes or until the grains are soft.

Soaking Put the bulgur in a deep bowl. Cover with hot water and mix with a fork. Leave to steep for 20 minutes, checking to make sure there is enough water. Drain and fluff up with a fork.

Cooking dried pasta

When cooking pasta, it is not necessary to add oil to the water unless you are cooking filled pasta such as ravioli (the oil will help prevent them from sticking together).

1 Heat the water with about 1 tsp salt per 100g (3½oz) of pasta. Cover the pan to speed up boiling.

2 When the water has reached a rolling boil, put in all the pasta.

3 Stir well for 30 seconds, to keep the pasta from sticking either to itself or the pan. Once boiling, set the timer for 2 minutes less than the recommended cooking time on the pack and cook uncovered.

4 Check the pasta when the timer goes off, then every 60 seconds until it is cooked al dente: tender, but with a little bite at the centre. Scoop out a cup of cooking water (it may be useful for loosening up a thick sauce).

5 Drain the pasta well in a colander. Transfer to a serving bowl, and use as required by your recipe.

Cooking fresh pasta

Fresh pasta is cooked in the same way as dried, but for a shorter time.

1 Bring the water to the boil.

2 Add the pasta to the boiling water and stir well. Set the timer for 2 minutes and keep testing every 30 seconds until the pasta is cooked al dente: tender, but with a little bite in the centre. Drain as above.

Perfect pasta

• Use about 1 litre (1¾ pints) of water per 100g (3½oz) of pasta.
• Rinse the pasta only if you are going to cool it for use in a salad, then drain well and toss with oil.
• If a recipe calls for cooking the pasta with the sauce after it has boiled, undercook the pasta slightly when boiling it.

Cooking other grains

Quinoa

This nutritious South American seed, which resembles a grain, makes a great alternative to rice.

1 Put the quinoa in a bowl of cold water. Mix well, soak for 2 minutes, then drain. Put in a pan with twice its volume of water. Bring to the boil.

2 Simmer for 10–20 minutes, according to the pack instructions. Remove from the heat, cover and leave to stand for 10 minutes.

Barley

There are three types of barley, all of which may be cooked on their own, or in a soup or stew.

Whole barley Soak the barley overnight in twice its volume of water, then drain well. Put the barley in a heavy-based pan, pour in boiling water and simmer for about 1½ hours or until tender. Check the liquid during cooking, adding more if necessary.

Scotch (pot) barley Rinse well, then simmer gently in boiling water for 45–50 minutes until tender.

Pearl barley This barley has had all of its outer husk removed, and needs no soaking. Rinse the barley and put it into a pan with twice its volume of water. Bring to the boil. Turn down the heat and simmer for 25–30 minutes until tender.

Cooking polenta

This classic Italian staple, made of ground cornmeal, may be cooked to make a grainy purée to be served immediately, or cooled and then fried or grilled.

Traditional polenta

1 Fill a pan with 1.2 litres (2 pints) water and add ¼ tsp salt. Pour in 225g (8oz) polenta and put the pan over a medium heat.

2 As the water starts to heat up, stir the polenta. Bring to the boil, reduce the heat to a simmer and continue cooking, stirring every few minutes, for 15-20 minutes until it comes away from the sides of the pan.

Perfect polenta

- Use coarse cornmeal if you want a slightly gritty texture, or fine cornmeal for a smooth texture.
- If you are serving traditional polenta straight from the pan, have all the other dishes ready – the polenta needs to be eaten straight away, otherwise it becomes thick and difficult to serve.

Baking polenta

1 Preheat the oven to 200°C (180°C fan oven) mark 6. Fill a pan with 1.2 litres (2 pints) water and add 1/4 tsp salt. Pour in 225g (8oz) polenta and put it over the heat. Bring to the boil, stirring, then simmer for 5 minutes.

2 Pour the polenta into an oiled baking dish, cover with foil and bake in the oven for 45–50 minutes. Brown under the grill.

Grilling polenta

1 Make traditional polenta (see left), then pour into an oiled baking dish. Smooth the surface with a spatula and leave to cool.

2 Cut the polenta into squares and brush the pieces with olive oil.

3 Preheat the grill or frying pan and cook for 5–10 minutes until hot and browned on both sides.

Ginger

1 **Grating** Cut off a piece of the root and peel with a vegetable peeler. Cut off any brown spots

2 Rest the grater on a board or small plate and grate the ginger. Discard any large fibres adhering to the pulp.

3 **Slicing, shredding and chopping** Cut slices off the ginger and cut off the skin carefully. Cut off any brown spots. Stack the slices and cut into shreds. To chop, stack the shreds and cut across into small pieces.

4 **Pressing** If you just need the juice from the ginger, peel and cut off any brown spots, then cut into small chunks and use a garlic press held over a small bowl to extract the juice.

Flavourings

Garlic is one of the most widely used flavourings around the world. Asian dishes often use garlic, ginger and spring onions as the basic flavourings. Spicier dishes may include chillies, lemongrass or a prepared spice paste such as Thai curry paste.

Spring onions

Cut off the roots and trim any coarse or withered green parts. Slice diagonally, or shred by cutting into 5cm (2in) lengths and then slicing down the lengths, or chop finely, according to the recipe.

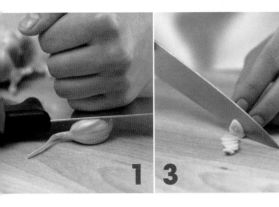

Garlic

1 Put the clove on a chopping board and place the flat side of a large knife on top of it. Press down firmly on the flat of the blade to crush the clove and break the papery skin.

2 Cut off the base of the clove and slip the garlic out of its skin. It should come away easily.

3 **Slicing** Using a rocking motion, with the knife tip on the board, slice the garlic as thinly as you need.

4 **Shredding and chopping** Holding the slices together, shred them across the slices. Chop the shreds if you need chopped garlic.

5 **Crushing** After step 2, the whole clove can be put into a garlic press. To crush with a knife: roughly chop the peeled cloves with a pinch of salt. Press down hard with the edge of a large knife (with the blade facing away from you), then drag the blade along the garlic while still pressing hard. Continue to do this, dragging the edge of the blade over the garlic.

Cook's Tip

Wash hands thoroughly after handling chillies – the volatile oils will sting if accidentally rubbed into your eyes.

Chillies

1 Cut off the cap and then slit open lengthways. Using a spoon, scrape out the seeds and the pith.

2 For diced chilli, cut into thin shreds lengthways, then cut crossways.

Food storage and hygiene

Storing food properly and preparing it in a hygienic way is important to ensure that food remains as nutritious and flavourful as possible, and to reduce the risk of food poisoning.

Hygiene

When you are preparing food, always follow these important guidelines:
Wash your hands thoroughly before handling food and again between handling different types of food, such as raw and cooked meat and poultry. If you have any cuts or grazes on your hands, be sure to keep them covered with a waterproof plaster.
Wash down worksurfaces regularly with a mild detergent solution or multi-surface cleaner.
Use a dishwasher if available. Otherwise, wear rubber gloves for washing-up, so that the water temperature can be hotter than unprotected hands can bear. Change drying-up cloths and cleaning cloths regularly. Note that leaving dishes to drain is more hygienic than drying them with a teatowel.
Keep raw and cooked foods separate, especially meat, fish and poultry. Wash kitchen utensils in between preparing raw and cooked foods. Never put cooked or ready-to-eat foods directly on to a surface that has just had raw fish, meat or poultry on it.
Keep pets out of the kitchen if possible; or make sure they stay away from worksurfaces. Never allow animals on to worksurfaces.

Shopping

Always choose fresh ingredients in prime condition from stores and markets that have a regular turnover of stock, to ensure that you buy the freshest produce possible.
Make sure items are within their 'best before' or 'use by' date. (Foods with a long shelf life have a 'best before' date; more perishable items have a 'use by' date.)
Pack frozen and chilled items in an insulated cool bag at the check-out and put them into the freezer or refrigerator as soon as you get home.
During warm weather in particular, buy perishable foods just before you return home. When packing items at the check-out, sort them according to where you will store them when you get home – the refrigerator, freezer, storecupboard, vegetable rack, fruit bowl, etc. This will make unpacking easier – and quicker.

The storecupboard

Although storecupboard ingredients will generally last a long time, correct storage is important:

Always check packaging for storage advice – even with familiar foods, because storage requirements may change if additives, sugar or salt have been reduced.

Check storecupboard foods for their 'best before' or 'use by' date and do not use them if the date has passed.

Keep all food cupboards scrupulously clean and make sure food containers and packets are properly sealed.

Once opened, treat canned foods as though fresh. Always transfer the contents to a clean container, cover and keep in the refrigerator. Similarly, jars, sauce bottles and cartons should be kept chilled after opening. (Check the label for safe storage times after opening.)

Transfer dry goods such as sugar, flour, rice and pasta to moisture-proof containers. When supplies are used up, wash the container well and dry thoroughly before refilling with new supplies.

Store oils in a dark cupboard away from any heat source, as heat and light can make them turn rancid and affect their colour. For the same reason, buy olive oil in dark green bottles.

Store vinegars in a cool place; they can turn bad in a warm environment.

Store dried herbs, spices and flavourings in a cool, dark cupboard or in dark jars. Buy in small quantities as their flavour will not last indefinitely.

Refrigerator storage

Fresh food needs to be kept in the cool temperature of the refrigerator to keep it in good condition and discourage the growth of harmful bacteria. Store day-to-day perishable items, such as opened jams and jellies, mayonnaise and bottled sauces, in the refrigerator along with eggs and dairy products, fruit juices, bacon, fresh and cooked meat (on separate shelves), and salads and vegetables (except potatoes, which don't suit being stored in the cold). A refrigerator should be kept at an operating temperature of 4–5°C.

It is worth investing in a refrigerator thermometer to check that the correct temperature is maintained. To ensure your refrigerator is functioning effectively for safe food storage, follow these guidelines:

To avoid bacterial cross-contamination, store cooked and raw foods on separate shelves, putting cooked foods on the top shelf. Ensure that all items are well wrapped.

Never put hot food into the refrigerator, as this will cause the internal temperature of the refrigerator to rise.

Avoid overfilling the refrigerator, as this restricts the circulation of air and prevents the appliance from working properly.

It can take some time for the refrigerator to return to the correct operating temperature once the door has been opened, so don't leave it open any longer than is necessary.

Clean the refrigerator regularly, using a specially formulated germicidal refrigerator cleaner. Alternatively, use a weak solution of bicarbonate of soda: 1 tbsp to 1 litre (1¾ pints) water.

If your refrigerator doesn't have an automatic defrost facility, defrost regularly.

Maximum refrigerator storage times

For pre-packed foods, always adhere to the 'use by' date on the packet. For other foods, the following storage times should apply, providing the food is in prime condition when it goes into the refrigerator and that your refrigerator is in good working order.

Vegetables and fruit

Green vegetables	3–4 days
Salad leaves	2–3 days
Hard and stone fruit	3–7 days
Soft fruit	1–2 days

Dairy food

Cheese, hard	1 week
Cheese, soft	2–3 days
Eggs	1 week
Milk	4–5 days

1

Salads and Light Lunches

Broad Bean, Pea and Mint Soup

1 tbsp olive oil

1 medium onion, finely chopped

1.1kg (2½lb) fresh broad beans (pre-podded weight), podded

700g (1½lb) fresh peas (pre-podded weight), podded

1.1 litres (2 pints) hot vegetable stock

2 tbsp freshly chopped mint, plus extra sprigs to garnish

3 tbsp crème fraîche, plus extra to garnish (optional)

salt and ground black pepper

1 Heat the oil in a large pan and fry the onion gently for 15 minutes until softened.

2 Meanwhile, blanch the broad beans by cooking them for 2–3 minutes in a large pan of boiling water. Drain and refresh under cold water. Slip the beans out of their skins.

3 Put the beans and peas into the pan with the onion and stir for 1 minute. Add the hot stock and bring to the boil. Simmer for 5–8 minutes until the vegetables are tender, then cool for a few minutes. Stir in the mint, then whizz in batches in a blender or food processor until smooth. Alternatively, use a stick blender.

4 Return the soup to the rinsed-out pan, stir in the crème fraîche and check the seasoning. Reheat gently, then ladle into warmed bowls and garnish with a little crème fraîche, if you like, and a sprig of mint.

Serves	EASY		NUTRITIONAL INFORMATION
4	**Preparation Time** 2 minutes	**Cooking Time** 30 minutes	**Per Serving** 176 calories, 4g fat (of which 1g saturates), 22g carbohydrate, 0.1g salt

Cook's Tips

Chillies vary enormously in strength, from quite mild to blisteringly hot, depending on the type of chilli and its ripeness. Taste a small piece first to check that it's not too hot for you.

Be extremely careful, when handling chillies, not to touch or rub your eyes with your fingers, as it will make them sting. Wash knives immediately after handling chillies. As a precaution, use rubber gloves when preparing them if you like.

Sweet Potato Soup

1 tbsp olive oil

1 large onion, finely chopped

2 tsp coriander seeds, crushed

2 red chillies, seeded and chopped (see Cook's Tips)

1 butternut squash, about 750g (1lb 11oz), peeled and roughly chopped

2 sweet potatoes, roughly chopped

2 tomatoes, peeled and diced

1.7 litres (3 pints) hot vegetable stock

salt and ground black pepper

1 Heat the oil in a large pan over a gentle heat and fry the onion for about 10 minutes until soft. Add the coriander seeds and chillies to the pan and cook for 1–2 minutes.

2 Add the squash, sweet potatoes and tomatoes and cook for 5 minutes. Add the hot stock, cover and bring to the boil. Simmer gently for 15 minutes or until the vegetables are soft. Using a blender, purée the soup in batches until smooth. Season with salt and pepper. Reheat gently, then divide among eight warmed bowls. Sprinkle with black pepper.

Serves 8	EASY		NUTRITIONAL INFORMATION	
	Preparation Time 20 minutes	**Cooking Time** 35 minutes	**Per Serving** 78 calories, 2g fat (of which trace saturates), 14g carbohydrate, 0.8g salt	Vegan Gluten free • Dairy free

175g (6oz) baby plum tomatoes, halved

2 small aubergines, thickly sliced

2 large yellow peppers, seeded and roughly chopped

2 red onions, cut into thin wedges

2 fat garlic cloves, crushed

5 tbsp olive oil

250g (9oz) couscous

400g can chopped tomatoes

2 tbsp harissa paste

25g (1oz) toasted pumpkin seeds (optional)

1 large bunch of coriander, roughly chopped

salt and ground black pepper

Summer Couscous

1 Preheat the oven to 230°C (210°C fan oven) mark 8. Put the vegetables and garlic into a large roasting tin, drizzle 3 tbsp oil over them and season with salt and pepper. Toss to coat. Roast for 20 minutes or until tender.

2 Meanwhile, put the couscous into a separate roasting tin and add 300ml (½ pint) cold water. Leave to soak for 5 minutes. Stir in the tomatoes and harissa and drizzle with the remaining oil. Pop in the oven next to the vegetables for 4–5 minutes to warm through.

3 Stir the pumpkin seeds, if you like, and the coriander into the couscous and season. Add the vegetables and stir.

EASY		NUTRITIONAL INFORMATION		Serves
Preparation Time 10 minutes	**Cooking Time** 20 minutes	**Per Serving** 405 calories, 21g fat (of which 3g saturates), 49g carbohydrate, 0.7g salt	Vegan Dairy free	**4**

Falafel, Rocket and Soured Cream Wraps

6 large flour tortillas

200g (7oz) soured cream

100g (3½oz) wild rocket

a small handful of fresh coriander, chopped

1 celery stick, finely chopped

180g pack ready-made falafel, roughly chopped or crumbled

1 Lay the tortillas on a board and spread each one with a little soured cream.

2 Divide the rocket among the wraps and sprinkle with coriander, celery and falafel.

3 Roll up as tightly as you can, then wrap each roll in clingfilm and chill for up to 3 hours or until ready to use. To serve, unwrap and cut each roll into quarters.

Serves 6	EASY		NUTRITIONAL INFORMATION
	Preparation Time 5 minutes, plus chilling		**Per Serving** 270 calories, 9g fat (of which 4g saturates), 42g carbohydrate, 0.5g salt

Try Something Different

Blend 25g (1oz) mild goat's cheese with 1 tbsp crème fraîche; put in the centre of the omelette before folding.

Classic French Omelette

2–3 medium eggs
1 tbsp milk or water
25g (1oz) unsalted butter
salt and ground black pepper
sliced or grilled tomatoes and freshly chopped flat-leafed parsley to serve

1 Whisk the eggs in a bowl, just enough to break them down – over-beating spoils the texture of the omelette. Season with salt and pepper and add the milk or water.

2 Heat the butter in an 18cm (7in) omelette pan or non-stick frying pan until it is foaming, but not brown. Add the eggs and stir gently with a fork or wooden spatula, drawing the mixture from the sides to the centre as it sets, and letting the liquid egg in the centre run to the sides. When set, stop stirring and cook for 30 seconds or until the omelette is golden brown underneath and still creamy on top: don't overcook. If you are making a filled omelette (see Try Something Different), add the filling at this point.

3 Tilt the pan away from you slightly and use a palette knife to fold one-third of the omelette to the centre, then fold over the opposite third. Slide the omelette out on to a warmed plate, letting it flip over so that the folded sides are underneath. Serve immediately, with tomatoes sprinkled with parsley.

EASY		NUTRITIONAL INFORMATION		Serves
Preparation Time 5 minutes	**Cooking Time** 5 minutes	**Per Serving** 449 calories, 40g fat (of which 19g saturates), 1g carbohydrate, 1g salt	Gluten free Dairy free	**1**

Cook's Tip

Raw garlic is renowned for its curative and protective powers, which include lowering blood pressure and cholesterol levels.

Fresh garlic has mild, juicy cloves and is available from May and throughout the summer. It is the classic form of garlic for making pesto, salsa verde, garlic mayonnaise and chilled soups.

Lemon Hummus with Black Olives

2 × 400g cans chickpeas, drained and rinsed

1 garlic clove (use fresh garlic when possible, see Cook's Tip), crushed

zest and juice of 1 lemon

4 tbsp olive oil

25g (1oz) pitted black olives, roughly chopped

1 tsp paprika, plus a little extra to sprinkle (optional)

sticks of raw vegetables and breadsticks to serve

1 Put the chickpeas and garlic into a food processor, add the lemon zest and juice and whizz to combine. With the motor running, drizzle in the oil to make a thick paste. If the hummus is too thick, add 1–2 tbsp cold water and whizz again.

2 Spoon into a bowl and stir in the olives and paprika. Sprinkle with a little extra paprika, if you like, and serve with raw vegetables and breadsticks for dipping.

Serves 4	EASY		NUTRITIONAL INFORMATION	
	Preparation Time 15 minutes		**Per Serving** 284 calories, 16g fat (of which 2g saturates), 25g carbohydrate, 1.2g salt	Vegan Gluten free • Dairy free

125g (4oz) plain flour, plus 2 tbsp extra to sprinkle

2 tbsp cornflour

2 tbsp arrowroot

125g (4oz) cauliflower, cut into small florets

2 large carrots, cut into matchsticks

16 button mushrooms

2 courgettes, sliced

2 red peppers, seeded and sliced

vegetable oil for deep-frying

salt and ground black pepper

fresh coriander sprigs to garnish

Vegetable Tempura

For the dipping sauce

25g (1oz) piece fresh root ginger, peeled and grated

4 tbsp dry sherry

3 tbsp soy sauce

1 Sift 125g (4oz) flour, the cornflour and arrowroot into a large bowl with a pinch each of salt and pepper. Gradually whisk in 300ml (½ pint) ice-cold water to form a thin batter. Cover and chill.

2 To make the dipping sauce, put the ginger, sherry and soy sauce into a heatproof bowl and pour in 200ml (7fl oz) boiling water. Stir well to mix, then put to one side.

3 Put the vegetables into a large bowl and sprinkle with 2 tbsp flour. Toss well to coat. Heat the oil in a wok or deep-fryer to 170°C (test by frying a small cube of bread: it should brown in 40 seconds).

4 Dip a handful of the vegetables in the batter, then remove with a slotted spoon, taking up a lot of the batter with the vegetables. Add to the hot oil and deep-fry for 3–5 minutes until crisp and golden. Remove with a slotted spoon and drain on kitchen paper; keep them hot while you cook the remaining batches. Serve immediately, garnished with coriander sprigs and accompanied by the dipping sauce.

A LITTLE EFFORT		NUTRITIONAL INFORMATION		Serves
Preparation Time 20 minutes	**Cooking Time** 15 minutes	**Per Serving** 450 calories, 21g fat (of which 3g saturates), 55g carbohydrate, 2.1g salt	Vegan Dairy free	4

Cook's Tip

If you can't find baby mozzarella, buy larger buffalo mozzarella instead – available from most major supermarkets – and cut it into large cubes.

Tomato, Mozzarella and Red Pesto Salad

225g (8oz) baby plum tomatoes, halved

225g (8oz) baby mozzarella, drained (see Cook's Tip)

100g jar red pepper pesto

175g (6oz) pitted black olives, drained

100g (3½oz) mixed salad leaves

salt and ground black pepper

1 Put the tomatoes, mozzarella, pesto and olives into a large bowl and toss together. Season with pepper. Check the seasoning before adding any salt, as the olives are already salty. Cover the bowl and put to one side.

2 Just before serving, toss the salad leaves with the tomato and mozzarella mixture.

Serves	EASY		NUTRITIONAL INFORMATION	
4	**Preparation Time** 10 minutes		**Per Serving** 400 calories, 36g fat (of which 12g saturates), 3g carbohydrate, 2.9g salt	Gluten free

Cook's Tip

Halloumi is a firm cheese made from ewe's milk. It is best used sliced and cooked.

Halloumi and Avocado Salad

250g (9oz) halloumi cheese, sliced into eight
(see Cook's Tip)

1 tbsp flour, seasoned

2 tbsp olive oil

200g (7oz) mixed leaf salad

2 ripe avocados, halved, stoned, peeled and sliced

fresh rocket leaves to garnish

lemon halves to serve

For the mint dressing

3 tbsp lemon juice

8 tbsp olive oil

3 tbsp freshly chopped mint

salt and ground black pepper

1 To make the dressing, whisk the lemon juice with the oil and mint, then season with salt and pepper.

2 Coat the halloumi with the flour. Heat the oil in a large frying pan and fry the cheese for 1 minute on each side or until a golden crust is formed.

3 Meanwhile, in a large bowl, add half the dressing to the salad leaves and avocado and toss together. Arrange the hot cheese on top and drizzle the remaining dressing over it. Garnish with rocket leaves and serve with lemon halves to squeeze over the salad.

EASY		NUTRITIONAL INFORMATION	Serves
Preparation Time 10 minutes	**Cooking Time** 2 minutes	**Per Serving** 397 calories, 34g fat (of which 13g saturates), 11g carbohydrate, 2.3g salt	**4**

Griddled Polenta with Gorgonzola Salad

2 tbsp olive oil, plus extra to grease

300ml (½ pint) semi-skimmed milk

10 sage leaves, roughly chopped

125g (4oz) quick-cook polenta

2 garlic cloves, crushed

25g (1oz) butter

100g (3½oz) salad leaves

125g (4oz) Gorgonzola cheese, cut into cubes

125g (4oz) each sunblush tomatoes and roasted red peppers

salt and ground black pepper

1 Lightly oil a 450g (1lb) loaf tin. Pour the milk into a pan, then add the sage, 1 scant tsp salt and 300ml (½ pint) water, and bring to the boil. Add the polenta to the pan in a thin, steady stream, stirring, to make a smooth paste.

2 Reduce the heat, add the garlic and cook for about 8 minutes, stirring occasionally. Add the oil, then season with pepper and stir well. Press into the prepared loaf tin, smooth the top and leave to cool for 45 minutes.

3 Once the polenta is cool, turn out on to a board and cut into eight slices.

4 Melt the butter in a griddle pan and fry the polenta slices on each side until golden. Divide among four plates. Add the salad leaves, Gorgonzola, sunblush tomatoes and peppers and serve.

EASY		NUTRITIONAL INFORMATION		Serves
Preparation Time 20 minutes, plus cooling	**Cooking Time** 20 minutes	**Per Serving** 362 calories, 22g fat (of which 11g saturates), 28g carbohydrate, 1.1g salt	Gluten free	**4**

Cook's Tip

Red bird's-eye chillies are always very hot. The smaller they are, the hotter they are.

Thai Noodle Salad

200g (7oz) sugarsnap peas, trimmed

250g pack Thai stir-fry rice noodles

100g (3½oz) cashew nuts

300g (11oz) carrots, peeled and cut into batons

10 spring onions, sliced diagonally

300g (11oz) bean sprouts

20g (¾oz) fresh coriander, roughly chopped, plus coriander sprigs to garnish

1 red bird's-eye chilli, seeded and finely chopped (see Cook's Tip and page 27)

2 tsp sweet chilli sauce

4 tbsp sesame oil

6 tbsp soy sauce

juice of 2 limes

salt and ground black pepper

1 Bring a pan of lightly salted water to the boil and blanch the sugarsnap peas for 2–3 minutes until just tender to the bite. Drain and refresh under cold water.

2 Put the noodles into a bowl, cover with boiling water and leave to soak for 4 minutes. Rinse under cold water and drain very well.

3 Toast the cashews in a dry frying pan until golden – about 5 minutes.

4 Put the sugarsnaps in a large glass serving bowl. Add the carrots, spring onions, bean sprouts, chopped coriander, chopped chilli, cashews and noodles. Mix together the chilli sauce, sesame oil, soy sauce and lime juice and season well with salt and pepper. Pour over the salad and toss together, then garnish with coriander sprigs and serve.

Serves 4	EASY		NUTRITIONAL INFORMATION	
	Preparation Time 20 minutes, plus soaking	**Cooking Time** 7–8 minutes	**Per Serving** 568 calories, 29g fat (of which 4g saturates), 65g carbohydrate, 2.9g salt	Vegan Dairy free

Warm Tofu, Fennel and Bean Salad

1 tbsp olive oil, plus 1 tsp

1 red onion, finely sliced

1 fennel bulb, finely sliced

1 tbsp cider vinegar

400g can butter beans, drained and rinsed

2 tbsp freshly chopped flat-leafed parsley

200g (7oz) smoked tofu

salt and ground black pepper

1 Heat 1 tbsp oil in a large frying pan. Add the onion and fennel and cook over a medium heat for 5–10 minutes until soft.

2 Add the vinegar and heat through for 2 minutes. Stir in the butter beans and parsley, season with salt and pepper, then tip into a bowl.

3 Slice the smoked tofu horizontally into four and then into eight triangles. Add to the pan with the remaining 1 tsp oil. Cook for 2 minutes on each side or until golden.

4 Divide the bean mixture among four plates, then add two slices of tofu to each plate.

EASY		NUTRITIONAL INFORMATION		Serves
Preparation Time 10 minutes	**Cooking Time** 15 minutes	**Per Serving** 150 calories, 6g fat (of which 1g saturates), 15g carbohydrate, 0.8g salt	Vegan Gluten free • Dairy free	**4**

Warm Pear and Walnut Caesar Salad

50g (2oz) walnut pieces

1 tbsp walnut or mild olive oil

a small knob of butter

3 firm rosy pears, quartered, cored and thickly sliced

1 bag Caesar salad with croutons, dressing and Parmesan

100g (3½oz) blue cheese, such as Roquefort, Stilton or Danish blue, crumbled (see as above)

1 bunch of chives, roughly chopped

1 Put the walnuts into a non-stick frying pan and dry-fry over a medium heat for about 1 minute until lightly toasted. Set aside.

2 Heat the oil and butter in the frying pan, then add the pears. Fry for 2 minutes on each side or until golden. Remove with a slotted spoon.

3 To serve, put the salad leaves into a large bowl. Add the walnuts, pears, croutons, Parmesan and blue cheese. Add the salad dressing and toss lightly, or serve the dressing separately in a small bowl. Serve immediately, garnished with chives.

Get Ahead

To prepare ahead Complete the recipe to the end of step 2, then leave the pears in the frying pan and set aside for up to 4 hours.

To use Warm the pears in the pan for 1 minute, then complete the recipe.

Serves	EASY		NUTRITIONAL INFORMATION
6	**Preparation Time** 10 minutes	**Cooking Time** 5 minutes	**Per Serving** 397 calories, 31g fat (of which 8g fat saturates), 19g carbohydrate, 1.3g salt

2

Pasta and Rice

Cook's Tip

Italian Dolcelatte cheese has a much milder flavour than Stilton or Roquefort; it also has a deliciously rich, creamy texture.

Spinach and Cheese Lasagne

125g (4oz) fresh or frozen leaf spinach, thawed

40g (1½oz) fresh basil, roughly chopped

250g (9oz) ricotta cheese

5 pieces marinated artichokes, drained and chopped

350g carton cheese sauce (see as above)

175g (6oz) Dolcelatte cheese, roughly diced (see Cook's Tip)

9 sheets fresh egg lasagne

25g (1oz) pinenuts, toasted

tomato salad to serve

1 Preheat the oven to 180°C (160°C fan oven) mark 4. Chop the spinach finely (if it was frozen, squeeze out the excess liquid first). Put into a bowl with the basil, ricotta cheese, artichokes and 6 tbsp cheese sauce. Mix well.

2 Beat the Dolcelatte into the remaining cheese sauce. Layer the ricotta mixture, lasagne, then cheese sauce into a 23 × 23cm (9 × 9in) ovenproof dish. Repeat to use up the remainder.

3 Cook the lasagne for 40 minutes. Sprinkle the pinenuts over the top and put back in the oven for a further 10–15 minutes until golden. Serve with a tomato salad.

Serves	EASY		NUTRITIONAL INFORMATION
6	**Preparation Time** 30 minutes	**Cooking Time** 50–55 minutes	**Per Serving** 442 calories, 27g fat (of which 14g saturates), 32g carbohydrate, 1.6g salt

Pappardelle with Spinach

350g (12oz) pappardelle pasta

350g (12oz) baby leaf spinach, roughly chopped

2 tbsp olive oil

75g (3oz) ricotta cheese

freshly grated nutmeg

salt and ground black pepper

1 Cook the pappardelle in a large pan of lightly salted boiling water, according to the pack instructions, until al dente.

2 Drain the pasta well, return to the pan and add the spinach, oil and ricotta, tossing for 10–15 seconds until the spinach has wilted. Season with a little nutmeg, salt and pepper and serve immediately.

EASY		NUTRITIONAL INFORMATION	Serves
Preparation Time 5 minutes	**Cooking Time** 12 minutes	**Per Serving** 404 calories, 11g fat (of which 3g saturates), 67g carbohydrate, 0.3g salt	**4**

Macaroni Cheese

500g (1lb 2oz) macaroni
500ml (18fl oz) crème fraîche
200g (7oz) freshly grated Parmesan
2 tbsp ready-made English or Dijon mustard
5 tbsp freshly chopped flat-leafed parsley
ground black pepper
green salad to serve

1 Cook the macaroni in a large pan of lightly salted boiling water according to the pack instructions. Drain and keep to one side.

2 Preheat the grill to high. Put the crème fraîche into a pan and heat gently. Stir in 175g (6oz) Parmesan, the mustard and parsley, and season well with black pepper. Stir the pasta into the sauce, spoon into bowls and sprinkle with the remaining cheese. Grill until golden and serve immediately with green salad.

Serves	EASY		NUTRITIONAL INFORMATION
4	**Preparation Time** 5 minutes	**Cooking Time** 15 minutes	**Per Serving** 1137 calories, 69g fat (of which 44g saturates), 96g carbohydrate, 2g salt

Pasta with Goat's Cheese and Sunblush Tomatoes

300g (11oz) conchiglie pasta

2 tbsp olive oil

1 red pepper, seeded and chopped

1 yellow pepper, seeded and chopped

½ tbsp sun-dried tomato paste

75g (3oz) sunblush tomatoes

75g (3oz) soft goat's cheese

2 tbsp freshly chopped parsley

salt and ground black pepper

1 Cook the pasta in a large pan of lightly salted boiling water, according to the pack instructions, until al dente.

2 Meanwhile, heat the oil in a pan and fry the red and yellow peppers for 5–7 minutes until softened and just beginning to brown. Add the tomato paste and cook for a further minute.

Add a ladleful of pasta cooking water to the pan and simmer for 1–2 minutes to make a sauce.

3 Drain the pasta and return to the pan. Pour the sauce on top, then add the tomatoes, goat's cheese and parsley. Toss together until the cheese begins to melt, then season with pepper and serve.

EASY		NUTRITIONAL INFORMATION	Serves
Preparation Time 5 minutes	**Cooking Time** 10 minutes	**Per Serving** 409 calories, 12g fat (of which 4g saturates), 64g carbohydrate, 0.4g salt	**4**

Cook's Tip

Fresh lasagne sheets wrapped around a filling are used here to make cannelloni, but you can also buy cannelloni tubes, which can easily be filled using a teaspoon.

Mixed Mushroom Cannelloni

6 sheets fresh lasagne

3 tbsp olive oil

1 small onion, finely sliced

3 garlic cloves, sliced

20g pack fresh thyme, finely chopped

225g (8oz) chestnut or brown-cap mushrooms, roughly chopped

125g (4oz) flat-cap mushrooms, roughly chopped

2 × 125g goat's cheese logs, with rind

350g carton cheese sauce

salt and ground black pepper

green salad to serve

1 Preheat the oven to 180°C (160°C fan oven) mark 4. Cook the lasagne in boiling water until just tender. Drain well and run it under cold water to cool. Keep covered with cold water until ready to use.

2 Heat the oil in a large pan and add the onion. Cook over a medium heat for 7–10 minutes until the onion is soft. Add the garlic and fry for 1–2 minutes. Keep a few slices of garlic to one side. Keep a little thyme for sprinkling later, then add the rest to the pan with the mushrooms. Cook for a further 5 minutes or until the mushrooms are golden brown and there is no excess liquid in the pan. Season, remove from the heat and put to one side.

3 Crumble one of the goat's cheese logs into the cooled mushroom mixture and stir together. Drain the lasagne sheets and pat dry with kitchen paper. Spoon 2–3 tbsp of the mushroom mixture along the long edge of each lasagne sheet, leaving a 1cm (½in) border. Roll up the pasta sheets and cut each roll in half. Put the pasta into a shallow ovenproof dish and spoon the cheese sauce over it. Slice the remaining goat's cheese into thick rounds and arrange across the middle of the pasta rolls. Sprinkle the reserved garlic and thyme on top. Cook in the oven for 30–35 minutes until golden and bubbling. Serve with a green salad.

Serves	A LITTLE EFFORT		NUTRITIONAL INFORMATION
4	**Preparation Time** 15 minutes	**Cooking Time** 50–55 minutes	**Per Serving** 631 calories, 37g fat (of which 18g saturates), 50g carbohydrate, 1.9g salt

Pea, Mint and Ricotta Pasta

300g (11oz) farfalle pasta
200g (7oz) frozen peas
175g (6oz) ricotta cheese
3 tbsp freshly chopped mint
2 tbsp extra virgin olive oil
salt and ground black pepper

1 Cook the pasta in a large pan of lightly salted boiling water, according to the pack instructions, until al dente. Add the frozen peas for the last 4 minutes of cooking.

2 Drain the pasta and peas, reserving a ladleful of pasta cooking water, then return to the pan. Stir in the ricotta and mint with the pasta water. Season well, drizzle with the oil and serve at once.

Serves	EASY		NUTRITIONAL INFORMATION
4	**Preparation Time** 5 minutes	**Cooking Time** 10 minutes	**Per Serving** 431 calories, 14g fat (of which 5g saturates), 63g carbohydrate, trace salt

Pesto Gnocchi

800g (1lb 12oz) fresh gnocchi

200g (7oz) green beans, trimmed and chopped

1 quantity of fresh Pesto (see page 17)

10 sunblush tomatoes, roughly chopped

1 Cook the gnocchi in a large pan of lightly salted boiling water, according to the pack instructions, or until all the gnocchi have floated to the surface. Add the beans to the water for the last 3 minutes of cooking time.

2 Drain the gnocchi and beans and put back into the pan. Add the pesto and tomatoes and toss well. Serve immediately.

EASY		NUTRITIONAL INFORMATION	Serves
Preparation Time 10 minutes	**Cooking Time** 10 minutes	**Per Serving** 579 calories, 30g fat (of which 4g saturates), 82g carbohydrate, 3.4g salt	**4**

Wild Mushroom Risotto

900ml (1½ pints) vegetable stock

6 tbsp olive oil

2 shallots, finely chopped

2 garlic cloves, finely chopped

2 tsp freshly chopped thyme, plus sprigs to garnish

1 tsp grated lemon zest

350g (12oz) risotto (arborio) rice

150ml (¼ pint) dry white wine

450g (1lb) mixed fresh mushrooms, such as oyster, shiitake and cep, sliced if large

1 tbsp freshly chopped flat-leafed parsley

salt and ground black pepper

1 Heat the stock in a pan to a steady, low simmer.

2 Meanwhile, heat half the oil in a heavy-based pan. Add the shallots, garlic, chopped thyme and lemon zest and fry gently for 5 minutes or until the shallots are softened. Add the rice and stir for 1 minute or until the grains are glossy. Add the wine, bring to the boil and let bubble until almost totally evaporated.

3 Gradually add the stock to the rice, a ladleful at a time, stirring with each addition and allowing it to be absorbed before adding more. Continue adding the stock slowly until the rice is tender. This should take about 25 minutes.

4 About 5 minutes before the rice is ready, heat the remaining oil in a large frying pan and stir-fry the mushrooms over a high heat for 4–5 minutes. Add to the rice with the parsley. The risotto should still be moist: if necessary, add a little more stock. Check the seasoning and serve at once, garnished with thyme sprigs.

Dos and Don'ts for the Perfect Risotto

Always use risotto (arborio) rice: the grains are thicker and shorter than long-grain rice and have a high starch content. They absorb liquid slowly, producing a creamy-textured risotto.

Stock should be hot when added: this swells the grains, yet keeps them firm. Keep stock simmering in a pan. Add it ladle by ladle to the risotto, allowing it to be absorbed by the rice after each addition.

The correct heat is vital. If the risotto gets too hot, the liquid evaporates too quickly and the rice won't cook evenly. If the heat is too low, the risotto will go gluey. Over a medium heat, the rice should cook in about 25 minutes.

Don't leave risotto – stir constantly to loosen the rice from the bottom of the pan.

The quantity of liquid given is approximate – adjust it so that, when cooked, the rice is tender but firm to the bite. It should be creamily bound together, neither runny nor dry.

EASY		NUTRITIONAL INFORMATION		Serves
Preparation Time 10 minutes	**Cooking Time** 30 minutes	**Per Serving** 341 calories, 12g fat (of which 2g saturates), 48g carbohydrate, 1g salt	Vegan Gluten free • Dairy free	**6**

Cook's Tip

If you can't find pumpkin, use butternut squash.

Pumpkin Risotto with Hazelnut Butter

50g (2oz) butter

175g (6oz) onion, finely chopped

900g (2lb) pumpkin, halved, peeled, seeded and cut into small cubes

2 garlic cloves, crushed

225g (8oz) risotto (arborio) rice

600ml (1 pint) hot vegetable stock

grated zest of ½ orange

40g (1½oz) Parmesan, shaved

salt and ground black pepper

For the hazelnut butter

50g (2oz) hazelnuts

125g (4oz) butter, softened

2 tbsp freshly chopped flat-leafed parsley

1 To make the hazelnut butter, spread the hazelnuts on a baking sheet and toast under a hot grill until golden brown, turning frequently. Put the nuts in a clean teatowel and rub off the skins, then chop finely. Put the nuts, butter and parsley on a piece of non-stick baking parchment. Season with pepper and mix together. Mould into a sausage shape, twist the baking parchment at both ends and chill.

2 To make the risotto, melt the butter in a large pan and fry the onion until soft but not coloured. Add the pumpkin and sauté over a low heat for 5–8 minutes until just beginning to soften. Add the garlic and rice and stir until well mixed. Increase the heat to medium and add the hot stock a little at a time, allowing the liquid to be absorbed after each addition. This will take about 25 minutes.

3 Stir in the orange zest and Parmesan and season with salt and pepper. Serve the risotto with a slice of the hazelnut butter melting on top.

Serves	EASY		NUTRITIONAL INFORMATION	
4	**Preparation Time** 15 minutes	**Cooking Time** 40 minutes	**Per Serving** 706 calories, 50g fat (of which 27g saturates), 51g carbohydrate, 1.1g salt	Gluten free

200g (7oz) long-grain rice

3 Chinese dried mushrooms, or 125g (4oz) button mushrooms, sliced

2 tbsp vegetable oil

4 spring onions, sliced diagonally into 2.5cm (1in) lengths

125g (4oz) canned bamboo shoots, drained and cut into 2.5cm (1in) strips

125g (4oz) bean sprouts

125g (4oz) frozen peas

2 tbsp soy sauce

3 medium eggs, beaten

fresh coriander sprigs to garnish

lime halves to serve

Vegetable Fried Rice

1 Put the rice into a pan and cover with enough cold water to come 2.5cm (1in) above the rice. Bring to the boil, then reduce the heat, cover tightly and simmer very gently for 20 minutes. Do not stir.

2 Remove the pan from the heat and leave to cool for 20 minutes, then cover with clingfilm and chill for 2–3 hours or overnight.

3 When ready to fry the rice, soak the dried mushrooms, if using, in warm water for about 30 minutes.

4 Drain the mushrooms, squeeze out excess moisture, then slice thinly.

5 Heat the oil in a wok or large frying pan over a high heat. Add the mushrooms, spring onions, bamboo shoots, bean sprouts and peas and stir-fry for 2–3 minutes. Add the soy sauce and cook briefly, stirring.

6 Fork up the rice, add it to the pan and stir-fry for 2 minutes. Pour in the eggs and continue to stir-fry for 2–3 minutes until the egg has scrambled and the rice is heated through. Serve immediately, garnished with coriander, with lime halves to squeeze over it.

EASY		NUTRITIONAL INFORMATION		Serves
Preparation Time 10 minutes, plus soaking and chilling	**Cooking Time** About 30 minutes	**Per Serving** 464 calories, 11g fat (of which 2g saturates), 76g carbohydrate, 1.5g salt	Dairy free	**4**

Get Ahead

To prepare ahead Fry the aubergine and onion as in step 1. Cover and keep in a cool place for 1½ hours.
To use Complete the recipe.

4–6 tbsp olive oil

275g (10oz) aubergine, roughly chopped

225g (8oz) onions, finely chopped

25g (1oz) butter

½ tsp cumin seeds

175g (6oz) long-grain rice

600ml (1 pint) vegetable stock

400g can chickpeas, drained and rinsed

225g (8oz) baby spinach leaves

salt and ground black pepper

Aubergine and Chickpea Pilau

1 Heat half the oil in a large pan or flameproof casserole over a medium heat. Fry the aubergine for 4–5 minutes, in batches, until a deep golden brown. Remove from the pan with a slotted spoon and put to one side. Add the remaining oil to the pan, then add the onions and cook for 5 minutes or until golden and soft.

2 Add the butter, then stir in the cumin seeds and rice. Fry for 1–2 minutes. Pour in the stock, season with salt and pepper and bring to the boil. Reduce the heat, then simmer, uncovered, for 10–12 minutes until most of the liquid has evaporated and the rice is tender.

3 Remove the pan from the heat. Stir in the chickpeas, spinach and reserved aubergine. Cover with a tight-fitting lid and leave to stand for 5 minutes until the spinach has wilted and the chickpeas are heated through. Adjust the seasoning to taste. Fork through the rice grains to separate and make the rice fluffy before serving.

Serves	EASY		NUTRITIONAL INFORMATION	
4	**Preparation Time** 10 minutes	**Cooking Time** 20 minutes, plus standing	**Per Serving** 462 calories, 20g fat (of which 5g saturates), 58g carbohydrate, 0.9g salt	Gluten free

Baked Stuffed Pumpkin

1 pumpkin, about 1.4–1.8kg (3–4lb)

2 tbsp olive oil

2 leeks, trimmed and chopped

2 garlic cloves, crushed

2 tbsp freshly chopped thyme leaves

2 tsp paprika

1 tsp turmeric

125g (4oz) long-grain rice, cooked

2 tomatoes, peeled, seeded and diced

50g (2oz) cashew nuts, toasted and roughly chopped

125g (4oz) Cheddar cheese, grated

salt and ground black pepper

1 Cut a 5cm (2in) slice from the top of the pumpkin and put to one side for the lid. Scoop out and discard the seeds. Using a knife and a spoon, cut out most of the pumpkin flesh, leaving a thin shell. Cut the pumpkin flesh into small pieces and put to one side.

2 Heat the oil in a large pan, add the leeks, garlic, thyme, paprika and turmeric and fry for 10 minutes. Add the chopped pumpkin flesh and fry for a further 10 minutes or until golden, stirring frequently to prevent sticking. Transfer the mixture to a bowl. Preheat the oven to 180°C (160°C fan oven) mark 4.

3 Add the pumpkin mixture to the cooked rice along with the tomatoes, cashews and cheese. Fork through to mix and season with salt and pepper.

4 Spoon the stuffing mixture into the pumpkin shell, top with the lid and bake for 1¼ –1½ hours until the pumpkin is softened and the skin is browned. Remove from the oven and leave to stand for 10 minutes. Cut into wedges to serve.

EASY		NUTRITIONAL INFORMATION		Serves
Preparation Time About 40 minutes	**Cooking Time** 1½ hours–1 hour 50 minutes, plus standing	**Per Serving** 438 calories, 24g fat (of which 9g saturates), 38g carbohydrate, 0.7g salt	Dairy free	**4**

Roasted Tomato Bulgur Salad

175g (6oz) bulgur wheat

700g (1½lb) cherry tomatoes or baby plum tomatoes

8 tbsp extra virgin olive oil

a handful each of mint and basil, roughly chopped, plus fresh basil sprigs to garnish

3–4 tbsp balsamic vinegar

1 bunch of spring onions, sliced

salt and ground black pepper

1 Put the bulgur wheat into a bowl and add boiling water to cover by 1cm (½in). Leave to soak for 30 minutes.

2 Preheat the oven to 220°C (200°C fan oven) mark 7. Put the tomatoes into a small roasting tin, drizzle with half the oil and add half the mint. Season with salt and pepper and roast for 10–15 minutes until beginning to soften.

3 Put the remaining oil and the vinegar into a large bowl. Add the warm pan juices from the roasted tomatoes and the soaked bulgur wheat.

4 Stir in the remaining chopped herbs and the spring onions and check the seasoning. You may need a little more vinegar, depending on the sweetness of the tomatoes.

5 Add the tomatoes and carefully toss to combine, then serve garnished with basil sprigs.

Cook's Tip

Bulgur wheat is widely used in Middle Eastern cooking and has a light, nutty flavour and texture. It is available in several different sizes – from coarse to fine.

Serves 6	EASY		NUTRITIONAL INFORMATION	
	Preparation Time 10 minutes, plus soaking	**Cooking Time** 10–15 minutes	**Per Serving** 258 calories, 16g fat (of which 2g saturates), 26g carbohydrate, 0.5g salt	Vegan Dairy free

3

Hearty Meals

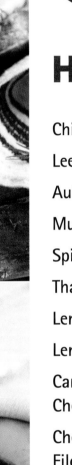

Chilli Bean Cake

3 tbsp olive oil

75g (3oz) wholemeal breadcrumbs

1 bunch of spring onions, finely chopped

1 orange pepper, seeded and chopped

1 small green chilli, seeded and finely chopped (see page 27)

1 garlic clove, crushed

1 tsp ground turmeric (optional)

400g can mixed beans, drained and rinsed

3 tbsp mayonnaise

a small handful of fresh basil, chopped

salt and ground black pepper

To serve

soured cream

freshly chopped coriander

lime wedges (optional)

1 Heat 2 tbsp oil in a non-stick frying pan over a medium heat and fry the breadcrumbs until golden and beginning to crisp. Remove and put to one side.

2 Add the remaining oil to the pan and fry the spring onions until soft and golden. Add the orange pepper, chilli, garlic and turmeric, if using. Cook, stirring, for 5 minutes.

3 Tip in the beans, mayonnaise, two-thirds of the fried breadcrumbs and the basil. Season with salt and pepper, mash roughly with a fork, then press the mixture down to flatten, and sprinkle with the remaining breadcrumbs. Fry the bean cake over a medium heat for 4–5 minutes until the base is golden. Remove from the heat, cut into wedges and serve with soured cream, coriander and the lime wedges, if you like.

Serves	EASY		NUTRITIONAL INFORMATION	
4	**Preparation Time** 10 minutes	**Cooking Time** 20 minutes	**Per Serving** 265 calories, 6g fat (of which 1g saturates), 41g carbohydrate, 2.1g salt	Dairy free

Try Something Different

Use sliced courgettes instead of aubergine.

Leek and Broccoli Bake

2 tbsp olive oil

1 large red onion, cut into wedges

1 aubergine, chopped

2 leeks, trimmed and cut into chunks

1 broccoli head, cut into florets and stalks chopped

3 large flat mushrooms, chopped

2 × 400g cans cherry tomatoes

3 rosemary sprigs, chopped

50g (2oz) Parmesan, freshly grated

salt and ground black pepper

1 Preheat the oven to 200°C (180°C fan oven) mark 6. Heat the oil in a large flameproof dish, add the onion, aubergine and leeks and cook for 10–12 minutes until golden and softened.

2 Add the broccoli, mushrooms, cherry tomatoes, half the rosemary and 300ml (½ pint) boiling water. Season with salt and pepper. Stir well, then cover and cook in the oven for 30 minutes.

3 Meanwhile, put the Parmesan into a bowl. Add the remaining rosemary and season with pepper. When the vegetables are cooked, remove the lid and sprinkle the Parmesan mixture on top. Cook, uncovered, in the oven for a further 5–10 minutes until the topping is golden.

Serves 4	EASY		NUTRITIONAL INFORMATION	
	Preparation Time 20 minutes	**Cooking Time** 45–55 minutes	**Per Serving** 245 calories, 13g fat (of which 4g saturates), 18g carbohydrate, 0.4g salt	Gluten free

Cook's Tip

Choose bags or bunches of fresh basil rather than a plant sold in a pot, as the leaves are larger and have a stronger, more peppery flavour.

Aubergine Parmigiana

2 large aubergines, thinly sliced lengthways

2 tbsp olive oil, plus extra to brush

3 fat garlic cloves, sliced

2 × 200ml tubs fresh Napoletana sauce

4 ready-roasted red peppers, roughly chopped

20g (¼oz) fresh basil, roughly chopped (see Cook's Tip)

150g (5oz) Taleggio or fontina cheese, coarsely grated

50g (2oz) Parmesan, coarsely grated

salt and ground black pepper

green salad to serve

1 Preheat the oven to 200°C (180°C fan oven) mark 6, and preheat the grill until hot. Put the aubergines on an oiled baking sheet, brush with oil, scatter with the garlic and season with salt and pepper. Grill for 5–6 minutes until golden.

2 Spread a little Napoletana sauce over the bottom of an oiled ovenproof dish, then cover with a layer of aubergine and peppers, packing the layers together as tightly as you can. Sprinkle a little basil and some of each cheese over the top. Repeat the layers, finishing with a layer of cheese. Season with pepper. Cook in the oven for 20 minutes or until golden. Serve hot with a green salad.

EASY		NUTRITIONAL INFORMATION		Serves
Preparation Time 10 minutes	**Cooking Time** About 25 minutes	**Per Serving** 432 calories, 28g fat (of which 11g saturates), 25g carbohydrate, 2.4g salt	Gluten free	**4**

Cook's Tip

Check the ingredients in the curry paste: some brands may not be suitable for vegetarians.

Mushroom and Bean Hotpot

3 tbsp olive oil

700g (1½lb) chestnut mushrooms, roughly chopped

1 large onion, finely chopped

2 tbsp plain flour

2 tbsp mild curry paste (see Cook's Tip)

150ml (¼ pint) dry white wine

400g can chopped tomatoes

2 tbsp sun-dried tomato paste

2 × 400g cans mixed beans, drained and rinsed

3 tbsp mango chutney

3 tbsp roughly chopped fresh coriander and mint

1 Heat the oil in a large pan over a low heat, then fry the mushrooms and onion until the onion is soft and dark golden. Stir in the flour and curry paste and cook for 1–2 minutes.

2 Add the wine, tomatoes, sun-dried tomato paste and beans and bring to the boil, then reduce the heat and simmer gently for 30 minutes, or until most of the liquid has reduced. Stir in the chutney and herbs before serving.

Serves	EASY		NUTRITIONAL INFORMATION	
6	**Preparation Time** 15 minutes	**Cooking Time** 30 minutes	**Per Serving** 280 calories, 10g fat (of which 1g saturates), 34g carbohydrate, 1.3g salt	Vegan

3 tbsp olive oil

2 small onions, sliced

2 garlic cloves, crushed

1 tbsp sweet paprika

1 small dried red chilli, seeded and finely chopped
(see page 27)

700g (1½lb) sweet potatoes, peeled and cubed

700g (1½lb) pumpkin, peeled and cut into chunks

125g (4oz) okra, trimmed

500g (1lb 2oz) passata

400g can haricot or cannellini beans, drained and rinsed

salt and ground black pepper

Spiced Bean and Vegetable Stew

1 Heat the oil in a large, heavy pan over a very gentle heat. Add the onion and garlic and cook for 5 minutes. Stir in the paprika and chilli and cook for a further 2 minutes.

2 Add the sweet potatoes, pumpkin, okra, passata and 900ml (1½ pints) water, and season generously with salt and pepper. Cover and bring to the boil, then reduce the heat and simmer for 20 minutes or until the vegetables are tender.

3 Add the haricot or cannellini beans and cook for 3 minutes to warm through. Serve immediately.

EASY		NUTRITIONAL INFORMATION		Serves
Preparation Time 5 minutes	**Cooking Time** About 30 minutes	**Per Serving** 262 calories, 7g fat (of which 1g saturates), 44g carbohydrate, 1.3g salt	Vegan Gluten free • Dairy free	**6**

Cook's Tip

Check the ingredients in the Thai curry paste: some contain shrimp and are therefore not suitable for vegetarians.

Try Something Different

Replace the carrots and/or broccoli with alternative vegetables – try baby sweetcorn, sugarsnap peas or mangetouts and simmer for only 5 minutes until tender.

Thai Vegetable Curry

2–3 tbsp red Thai curry paste (see Cook's Tip)

2.5cm (1in) piece fresh root ginger, peeled and finely chopped

50g (2oz) cashew nuts

400ml can coconut milk

3 carrots, cut into thin batons

1 broccoli head, cut into florets

20g (¼ oz) fresh coriander, roughly chopped

zest and juice of 1 lime

2 large handfuls of spinach leaves

basmati rice to serve

1 Put the curry paste into a large pan, add the ginger and cashew nuts and stir-fry over a medium heat for 2–3 minutes.

2 Add the coconut milk, cover and bring to the boil. Stir the carrots into the pan, then reduce the heat and simmer for 5 minutes. Add the broccoli florets and simmer for a further 5 minutes or until tender.

3 Stir the coriander and lime zest into the pan with the spinach. Squeeze the lime juice over the curry and serve with basmati rice.

Serves 4	EASY		NUTRITIONAL INFORMATION	
	Preparation Time 10 minutes	**Cooking Time** 15 minutes	**Per Serving** 200 calories, 10g fat (of which 2g saturates), 19g carbohydrate, 0.7g salt	Vegan Gluten free • Dairy free

2 tbsp olive oil

2 onions, sliced

4 carrots, sliced

3 leeks, trimmed and sliced

450g (1lb) button mushrooms

2 garlic cloves, crushed

2.5cm (1in) piece fresh root ginger, peeled and grated

1 tbsp ground coriander

225g (8oz) split red lentils, rinsed and drained

750ml (1¼ pints) hot vegetable stock

4 tbsp freshly chopped coriander

salt and ground black pepper

Lentil Casserole

1 Preheat the oven to 180°C (160°C fan oven) mark 4. Heat the oil in a flameproof casserole, add the onions, carrots and leeks and fry, stirring, for 5 minutes. Add the mushrooms, garlic, ginger and ground coriander and fry for 2–3 minutes.

2 Stir the lentils into the casserole with the hot stock. Season with salt and pepper and return to the boil. Cover and cook in the oven for 45–50 minutes until the vegetables and lentils are tender. Stir in the chopped coriander before serving.

EASY		NUTRITIONAL INFORMATION		Serves
Preparation Time 20 minutes	**Cooking Time** 1 hour	**Per Serving** 239 calories, 6g fat (of which 1g saturates), 36g carbohydrate, 0.4g salt	Vegan Gluten free • Dairy free	**6**

Cook's Tip

Oil-water spray is far lower in calories than oil alone and, as it sprays on thinly and evenly, you'll use less. Fill one-eighth of a travel-sized spray bottle with oil such as sunflower, light olive or vegetable (rapeseed) oil, then top up with water. To use, shake well before spraying. Store in the fridge.

oil-water spray (see Cook's Tip)

2 red onions, chopped

1½ tsp each ground coriander and ground cumin

½ tsp ground paprika

2 garlic cloves, crushed

2 sun-dried tomatoes, chopped

¼ tsp crushed dried chilli flakes

125ml (4fl oz) red wine

300ml (½ pint) hot vegetable stock

2 × 400g cans brown or green lentils, drained and rinsed

2 × 400g cans chopped tomatoes

sugar to taste

salt and ground black pepper

natural low-fat yogurt or soya yogurt and rice to serve

Lentil Chilli

1 Spray a saucepan with the oil-water spray and cook the onions for 5 minutes or until softened. Add the coriander, cumin and paprika. Combine the garlic, sun-dried tomatoes, chilli, wine and hot stock and add to the pan. Cover and simmer for 5–7 minutes. Uncover and simmer until the onions are very tender and the liquid has almost gone.

2 Stir in the lentils and canned tomatoes and season with salt and pepper. Simmer, uncovered, for 15 minutes or until thick. Stir in sugar to taste. Remove from the heat.

3 Ladle out a quarter of the mixture and whizz in a food processor or blender. Combine the puréed and unpuréed portions. Serve with yogurt and rice.

Serves 6	EASY		NUTRITIONAL INFORMATION	
	Preparation Time 10 minutes	**Cooking Time** 30 minutes	**Per Serving** 195 calories, 2g fat (of which trace saturates), 32g carbohydrate, 0.1g salt	Vegan Gluten free • Dairy free

Caramelised Onion and Goat's Cheese Tart

230g ready-made shortcrust pastry case

275g jar onion confit

300g (11oz) mild soft goat's cheese

1 medium egg, beaten

25g (1oz) freshly grated Parmesan

50g (2oz) wild rocket

balsamic vinegar and extra virgin olive oil to drizzle

salt and ground black pepper

1 Preheat the oven to 200°C (180°C fan oven) mark 6. Line the pastry case with greaseproof paper, fill with baking beans and bake blind for 10 minutes. Remove the paper and beans, prick the pastry base all over with a fork and bake for a further 15–20 minutes until golden.

2 Spoon the onion confit into the pastry case. Beat the goat's cheese and egg together in a bowl until smooth, season with salt and pepper, then spoon on top of the onions. Level the surface with a knife and sprinkle the Parmesan all over. Cook the tart for 25–30 minutes until the filling is set and just beginning to turn golden.

3 Leave to cool for 15 minutes, then cut away the sides of the foil case and carefully slide the tart on to a plate. Just before serving, arrange the rocket on top of the tart and drizzle with vinegar and oil. Serve warm.

EASY		NUTRITIONAL INFORMATION	Serves
Preparation Time 10 minutes	**Cooking Time** 1 hour	**Per Serving** 480 calories, 28g fat (of which 14g saturates), 44g carbohydrate, 1.5g salt	**6**

Chestnut and Butternut Squash Filo Parcels

½ tbsp olive oil

75g (3oz) butter

½ onion, finely chopped

5 fresh rosemary sprigs

½ small butternut squash, peeled and finely chopped

1 celery stalk, finely chopped

½ firm pear, finely chopped

100g (3½oz) peeled, cooked (or vacuum-packed) chestnuts, roughly chopped

1 slice walnut bread, about 50g (2oz), cut into small cubes

8 sheets filo pastry, about 30.5 × 20.5cm (12 × 8in) each

50g (2oz) cream cheese

salt and ground black pepper

1 Heat the oil and 15g (½oz) butter in a medium pan, add the onion and fry gently for 10 minutes. Finely chop one rosemary sprig and add to the pan, along with the squash. Continue to cook for 5 minutes or until everything is soft and golden. Add the celery and pear and cook for 1–2 minutes. Add the chestnuts, season and mix well. Add the bread to the pan, mix everything together, then set aside to cool.

2 Preheat the oven to 200°C (180°C fan oven) mark 6. Melt the remaining butter in a pan. Brush one sheet of filo pastry with the melted butter and layer another sheet of pastry on top, diagonally. Put a quarter of the chestnut mixture in the centre of the pastry and dot with a quarter of the cream cheese. Brush the edges of the pastry with a little more butter, bring the edges up and over the filling and pinch together tightly to make a parcel. Repeat to make three more parcels.

3 Put the parcels on a lightly greased baking sheet and cook for 25–30 minutes until the pastry is golden and the filling is piping hot; 5 minutes before the end of the cooking time, put a rosemary sprig into the top of each parcel. Serve hot.

Freezing Tip

To freeze Complete the recipe to the end of step 2, put the parcels in a freezer-proof container and freeze for up to one month.

To use Cook from frozen in a preheated oven at 200°C (180°C fan oven) mark 6 for 30 minutes, or until the pastry is golden. Complete the recipe.

Serves	EASY		NUTRITIONAL INFORMATION
4	**Preparation Time** 40 minutes	**Cooking Time** 45–50 minutes	**Per Serving** 408 calories, 22g fat (of which 13g saturates), 49g carbohydrate, 0.5g salt

Cheese Fondue Tarts

butter to grease

flour to dust

425g pack puff pastry, thawed if frozen

200g (7oz) each Jarlsberg and Gouda cheese, grated

1 garlic clove, crushed

150ml (¼ pint) single cream

juice of 1 small lemon

½ tsp paprika

2 tsp cornflour

50ml (2fl oz) vodka

2 tbsp freshly chopped dill, plus extra to garnish

1 Preheat the oven to 220°C (200°C fan oven) mark 7 and grease a 12-cup bun tin or muffin pan. On a lightly floured surface, roll out the pastry to 3mm (⅛in) thick. Cut out twelve 10cm (4in) rounds and put into the tin. Prick the bases and chill for 10 minutes. Line with greaseproof paper and fill with baking beans. Bake for 15–20 minutes, then remove the paper and beans and bake for 5 minutes or until golden.

2 Meanwhile, put the cheese, garlic, cream, lemon juice and paprika into a pan and heat, stirring, to make a smooth sauce. Mix the cornflour with the vodka, add to the pan and cook for 1–2 minutes. Stir in the dill.

3 Spoon the mixture into the pastry cases, scatter with dill and serve warm.

Serves	EASY		NUTRITIONAL INFORMATION
6	**Preparation Time** 20 minutes, plus chilling	**Cooking Time** 25 minutes	**Per Serving** 337 calories, 22g fat (of which 3g saturates), 28g carbohydrate, 0.6g salt

1 tbsp vegetable oil

1 onion, finely chopped

1 garlic clove, crushed

1 tbsp cumin seeds

400g (14oz) baby leaf spinach

1.1kg (2½lb) waxy potatoes, such as Desirée, boiled until tender, cooled, peeled and sliced

2 × 200g packs feta cheese, crumbled

2 medium eggs, beaten

200g pack filo pastry, thawed if frozen

50g (2oz) butter, melted

salt and ground black pepper

Spinach and Feta Pie

1 Heat the oil in a large pan and cook the onion for 10 minutes until soft. Add the garlic and cumin and cook for 1–2 minutes. Add the spinach, cover and cook until the spinach has just wilted – 1–2 minutes. Tip into a bowl and allow to cool. Add the potatoes, cheese and eggs, then season and mix.

2 Preheat the oven to 200°C (180°C fan oven) mark 6. Lightly butter a 28cm (11in) tart tin. Unroll the pastry and cut the sheets lengthways into three. Work with one-third of the strips at a time and cover the remainder with clingfilm. Lay a strip on the tin, starting from the middle so that half covers the tin and half hangs over the edge. Brush with melted butter, then lay another strip next to it, slightly overlapping, and brush again. Repeat, working quickly around the tin in a cartwheel shape.

3 Add the filling and level the surface. Fold the overhanging pastry to cover the mixture, filling any gaps with leftover pastry. Drizzle with the remaining melted butter, then cook for 45 minutes or until golden.

EASY		NUTRITIONAL INFORMATION	Serves
Preparation Time 40 minutes, plus cooling	**Cooking Time** 45 minutes	**Per Serving** 311 calories, 15g fat (of which 9g saturates), 33g carbohydrate, 1.7g salt	**10**

Easy Leek Pie

275g (10oz) plain flour, plus extra to dust

1 tsp English mustard powder

175g (6oz) cold butter, cut into cubes

50g (2oz) mature Cheddar cheese, grated

2 egg yolks, lightly beaten

900g (2lb) leeks, cut into 1cm (½in) slices, washed and drained

2 medium red onions, each cut into 8 wedges

juice of ½ lemon

leaves of 5 thyme sprigs

4 tbsp olive oil

1 small egg, lightly beaten

salt and ground black pepper

seasonal vegetables to serve

1 Put the flour, mustard powder, butter and ½ tsp salt into a food processor. Pulse until the mixture forms crumbs, then add the cheese, egg yolks and 2–3 tbsp cold water. Process briefly until the mixture comes together, then form into a ball, wrap in clingfilm and put in the freezer for 10 minutes.

2 Preheat the oven to 200°C (180°C fan oven) mark 6. Cook the leeks with 3 tbsp water in a covered pan until softened. Drain and set aside. Gently cook the onions and lemon juice in a covered pan until softened.

3 Roll out the pastry on a large, lightly floured sheet of baking parchment, to a 38cm (15in) round. Lift paper and pastry on to a baking sheet. Put the onions and leeks in the centre of the pastry, leaving a 7.5cm (3in) border. Sprinkle with the thyme, season with salt and pepper and drizzle with the oil. Fold the pastry edges over the filling. Brush the pastry rim with beaten egg. Bake for 50 minutes or until the vegetables are tender. Serve with vegetables.

EASY		NUTRITIONAL INFORMATION	Serves
Preparation Time 15 minutes	**Cooking Time** 1 hour	**Per Serving** 571 calories, 39g fat (of which 20g saturates), 45g carbohydrate, 0.7g salt	**6**

4

Cooking for Friends

White Nut Roast

40g (1½oz) butter

1 onion, finely chopped

1 garlic clove, crushed

225g (8oz) mixed white nuts, such as brazils, macadamias, pinenuts and whole almonds, ground in a food processor

125g (4oz) fresh white breadcrumbs

grated zest and juice of ½ lemon

75g (3oz) sage Derby cheese or Parmesan, grated

125g (4oz) cooked, peeled (or vacuum-packed) chestnuts, roughly chopped

½ × 400g can artichoke hearts, roughly chopped

1 medium egg, lightly beaten

2 tsp each freshly chopped parsley, sage and thyme, plus extra sprigs

salt and ground black pepper

1 Preheat the oven to 200°C (180°C fan oven) mark 6. Melt the butter in a pan and cook the onion and garlic for 5 minutes or until soft. Put into a large bowl and set aside to cool.

2 Add the nuts, breadcrumbs, zest and juice of the lemon, cheese, chestnuts and artichokes. Season well and bind together with the egg. Stir in the chopped herbs.

3 Put the mixture on a large piece of buttered foil and shape into a fat sausage, packing tightly. Scatter with the extra herb sprigs and wrap in the foil.

4 Cook on a baking sheet for 35 minutes, then unwrap the foil slightly and cook for a further 15 minutes until turning golden.

Freezing Tip

To freeze Complete the recipe to the end of step 3, cool, cover and freeze for up to one month.

To use Cook from frozen for 45 minutes, then unwrap the foil slightly and cook for a further 15 minutes until turning golden.

Serves	EASY		NUTRITIONAL INFORMATION
8	**Preparation Time** 20 minutes	**Cooking Time** About 1 hour	**Per Serving** 371 calories, 28g fat (of which 9g saturates), 20g carbohydrate, 0.8g salt

Get Ahead

To prepare ahead Complete the recipe to the end of step 4, up to one day ahead. Cover and chill.
To use Reheat under the grill for 5 minutes.

40g (1½oz) butter

4 Romano peppers, halved, with stalks on and seeded

3 tbsp olive oil

350g (12oz) chestnut mushrooms, roughly chopped

4 tbsp finely chopped fresh chives

100g (3½oz) feta cheese

50g (2oz) fresh white breadcrumbs

25g (1oz) freshly grated Parmesan

salt and ground black pepper

Roasted Stuffed Peppers

1 Preheat the oven to 180°C (160°C fan oven) mark 4. Use a little of the butter to grease a shallow ovenproof dish and put the peppers in it side by side, ready to be filled.

2 Heat the remaining butter and 1 tbsp oil in a pan. Add the mushrooms and fry until they're golden and there's no excess liquid left in the pan. Stir in the chives, then spoon the mixture into the pepper halves.

3 Crumble the feta over the mushrooms. Mix the breadcrumbs and Parmesan in a bowl, then sprinkle over the peppers.

4 Season with salt and pepper and drizzle with the remaining oil. Roast in the oven for 45 minutes or until golden and tender. Serve warm.

Serves 8	EASY		NUTRITIONAL INFORMATION
	Preparation Time 20 minutes	**Cooking Time** 45 minutes	**Per Serving** 189 calories, 14g fat (of which 6g saturates), 11g carbohydrate, 0.9g salt

Stuffed Aubergines

4 small aubergines

2 tbsp olive oil

25g (1oz) butter

1 small onion, very finely chopped

4 small, ripe tomatoes, peeled and roughly chopped

2 tsp chopped fresh basil or 1 tsp dried basil

2 medium eggs, hard-boiled and roughly chopped

1 tbsp capers

225g (8oz) fontina or Gruyère cheese, sliced

salt and ground black pepper

couscous with herbs, to serve

1 Cut the aubergines in half lengthways and scoop out the flesh. Put the aubergine shells to one side.

2 Chop the aubergine flesh finely, then spread out on a plate and sprinkle with salt. Leave to stand for 20 minutes (this removes the bitter flavour), then turn into a colander. Rinse, drain and dry. Preheat the oven to 180°C (160°C fan oven) mark 4.

3 Heat half the oil in a frying pan with the butter, add the onion and fry gently for 5 minutes until soft but not coloured. Add the tomatoes, basil, and salt and pepper to taste.

4 Meanwhile, put the aubergine shells in a single layer in an oiled ovenproof dish. Brush the insides with the remaining oil, then bake in the oven for 10 minutes.

5 Spoon half the tomato mixture into the aubergine shells. Cover with a layer of egg, capers, then a layer of cheese. Spoon the remaining tomato mixture over the top. Bake for a further 15 minutes and serve sizzling hot with couscous.

EASY		NUTRITIONAL INFORMATION	Serves
Preparation Time 10 minutes, plus standing	**Cooking Time** 30 minutes	**Per Serving** 367 calories, 28g fat (of which 14g saturates), 8g carbohydrate, 1.7g salt	**4**

Try Something Different

Try marinated peppers, artichokes or chargrilled aubergines instead of the olives and sunblush tomatoes.

Deli Pizza

6 tbsp tomato pizza sauce

2 pizzeria-style pizza bases

100g (3½oz) soft goat's cheese

1 red onion, finely sliced

100g (3½oz) sunblush tomatoes

100g (3½oz) pitted black olives

a handful of fresh basil, roughly torn

green salad to serve

1 Preheat the oven to 220°C (200°C fan oven) mark 7. Put a large baking sheet on the top shelf to heat up.

2 Spread a thin layer of the tomato sauce over each of the pizza bases, leaving a 2.5cm (1in) border around the edge. Top with dollops of goat's cheese, then scatter the red onion, tomatoes and olives over it.

3 Slide one of the pizzas on to the hot baking sheet and bake for 15 minutes or until golden and crisp. Repeat with the second pizza base. Scatter the torn basil over each pizza and serve immediately with a green salad.

Serves 4	EASY		NUTRITIONAL INFORMATION
	Preparation Time 5 minutes	**Cooking Time** 15 minutes	**Per Serving** 440 calories, 15g fat (of which 5g saturates), 64g carbohydrate, 2.8g salt

Try Something Different

Replace half the aubergines with 400g (14oz) courgettes; use a mix of green and red peppers; garnish with fresh basil instead of thyme.

400g (14oz) red peppers, seeded and roughly chopped

700g (1½lb) aubergines, stalk removed, cut into chunks

450g (1lb) onions, peeled and cut into wedges

4 or 5 garlic cloves, unpeeled and left whole

150ml (¼ pint) olive oil

1 tsp fennel seeds

200ml (7fl oz) passata

sea salt and ground black pepper

a few fresh thyme sprigs to garnish

Roasted Ratatouille

1 Preheat the oven to 240°C (220°C fan oven) mark 9. Put the peppers, aubergine, onions, garlic, oil and fennel seeds into a roasting tin. Season with sea salt flakes and pepper and toss together.

2 Transfer to the oven and cook for 30 minutes (tossing frequently during cooking), or until the vegetables are charred and beginning to soften.

3 Stir the passata through the vegetables and put the roasting tin back in the oven for 50–60 minutes, stirring occasionally. Garnish with the thyme sprigs and serve.

EASY		NUTRITIONAL INFORMATION		Serves
Preparation Time 15 minutes	**Cooking Time** 1½ hours	**Per Serving** 236 calories, 19g fat (of which 3g saturates), 14g carbohydrate, 0.5g salt	Vegan Gluten free • Dairy free	**6**

Try Something Different

Use sliced sweet potatoes, or butternut squash, seeded and cut into chunks, instead of the potatoes.

450g (1lb) potatoes, peeled and cut lengthways into 5mm (¼in) slices

1 aubergine, sliced into rounds

1 large red onion, cut into wedges

2 red peppers, seeded and sliced

4 tbsp olive oil

2 tbsp chopped thyme

225g (8oz) tomatoes, thickly sliced

2 garlic cloves, sliced

250g (9oz) passata

250g (9oz) soft goat's cheese

300g (11oz) natural yogurt

3 medium eggs

25g (1oz) Parmesan, grated

salt and ground black pepper

green salad to serve

Vegetable Moussaka

1 Preheat the oven to 230°C (210°C fan oven) mark 8. Boil the potatoes in a pan of lightly salted water for 5 minutes. Drain and put into a large roasting tin with the aubergine, onion and peppers. Drizzle with oil, add the thyme, toss and season with salt and pepper. Roast for 30 minutes, stirring occasionally.

2 Add the tomatoes and garlic and roast for 15 minutes, then take out of the oven. Reduce the oven temperature to 200°C (180°C fan oven) mark 6.

3 Put half the vegetables into a 1.7 litre (3 pint) ovenproof dish, then spoon half the passata over them and spread the goat's cheese on top. Repeat with the rest of the vegetables and passata. Mix together the yogurt, eggs and Parmesan. Season and then pour over the top. Cook in the oven for 45 minutes or until heated through. Serve with a green salad.

Serves 6	EASY		NUTRITIONAL INFORMATION
	Preparation Time 45 minutes	**Cooking Time** About 1½ hours	**Per Serving** 399 calories, 24g fat (of which 11g saturates), 29g carbohydrate, 1.2g salt

Try Something Different

Replace half the black-eyed beans with red kidney beans.

Black-eyed Bean Chilli

1 tbsp olive oil

1 onion, chopped

3 celery sticks, finely chopped

2 × 400g cans black-eyed beans, drained and rinsed

2 × 400g cans chopped tomatoes

2 or 3 splashes of Tabasco sauce

3 tbsp freshly chopped coriander

4 warmed tortillas and soured cream to serve

1 Heat the oil in a frying pan. Add the onion and celery and cook for 10 minutes until softened.

2 Add the beans, tomatoes and Tabasco to the pan. Bring to the boil, then reduce the heat and simmer for 10 minutes.

3 Just before serving, stir in the coriander. Spoon the chilli on to the warm tortillas, roll up and serve with soured cream.

EASY		NUTRITIONAL INFORMATION	Serves
Preparation Time 10 minutes	**Cooking Time** 20 minutes	**Per Serving** 245 calories, 5g fat (of which 1g saturates), 39g carbohydrate, 1.8g salt	**4**

Curried Tofu Burgers

1 tbsp sunflower oil, plus extra to fry

1 large carrot, finely grated

1 large onion, finely grated

2 tsp coriander seeds, finely crushed (optional)

1 garlic clove, crushed

1 tsp curry paste (see Cook's Tip, page 74)

1 tsp tomato purée

225g pack firm tofu

25g (1oz) fresh wholemeal breadcrumbs

25g (1oz) mixed nuts, finely chopped

plain flour to dust

salt and ground black pepper

rice and green vegetables to serve

1 Heat the oil in a large frying pan. Add the carrot and onion and fry for 3–4 minutes until the vegetables are softened, stirring all the time. Add the coriander seeds, if using, and the garlic, curry paste and tomato purée. Increase the heat and cook for 2 minutes, stirring all the time.

2 Put the tofu into a bowl and mash with a potato masher. Stir in the vegetables, breadcrumbs and nuts and season with salt and pepper. Beat thoroughly until the mixture starts to stick together. With floured hands, shape the mixture into eight burgers.

3 Heat some oil in a frying pan and fry the burgers for 3–4 minutes on each side until golden brown. Alternatively, brush lightly with oil and cook under a hot grill for about 3 minutes on each side or until golden brown. Drain on kitchen paper and serve hot, with rice and green vegetables.

Serves	EASY		NUTRITIONAL INFORMATION	
4	**Preparation Time** 20 minutes	**Cooking Time** 6–8 minutes	**Per Serving** 253 calories, 18g fat (of which 3g saturates), 15g carbohydrate, 0.2g salt	Vegan

2 tbsp sunflower oil

1 onion, sliced

2 garlic cloves, crushed

½ tsp hot chilli powder, plus extra to garnish

1 tsp each ground coriander and ground cumin

1 tbsp tomato purée

400g can chopped tomatoes

200g can red kidney beans, drained and rinsed

400g can borlotti beans, drained and rinsed

400g can flageolet beans, drained and rinsed

150ml (¼ pint) hot vegetable stock

2 ripe avocados

juice of ½ lime, plus lime wedges to serve

1 tbsp freshly chopped coriander, plus sprigs to garnish

6 ready-made flour tortillas

150ml (¼ pint) soured cream

salt and ground black pepper

Spicy Bean and Tomato Fajitas

1 Heat the oil in a large pan, add the onion and cook gently for 5 minutes. Add the garlic and spices and cook for a further 2 minutes.

2 Add the tomato purée and cook for 1 minute, then add the tomatoes, beans and hot stock. Season well with salt and pepper and bring to the boil, then reduce the heat and simmer for 15 minutes, stirring occasionally.

3 Halve, stone and peel the avocados, then chop. Put the avocado into a bowl, add the lime juice and chopped coriander and mash. Season to taste.

4 Warm the tortillas: either wrap them in foil and heat in the oven at 180°C (160°C fan oven) mark 4 for 10 minutes, or put on to a plate and microwave on full power for 45 seconds (based on a 900W oven).

5 Spoon some beans down the centre of each tortilla. Fold up the bottom to keep the filling inside, then wrap the sides in so they overlap. Spoon on the avocado and soured cream. Sprinkle with chilli powder and coriander sprigs; serve with lime wedges.

Serves 6	EASY		NUTRITIONAL INFORMATION
	Preparation Time 15 minutes	**Cooking Time** 25 minutes	**Per Serving** 512 calories, 20g fat (of which 6g saturates), 71g carbohydrate, 1.5g salt

Try Something Different

Use a different cheese, such as Stilton.

Spinach and Goat's Cheese Frittata

200g (7oz) baby leeks, trimmed and chopped

4 spring onions, chopped

125g (4oz) baby leaf spinach

6 large eggs

4 tbsp milk

freshly grated nutmeg

125g (4oz) soft goat's cheese, chopped (see Cook's Tip)

1 tbsp olive oil

salt and ground black pepper

mixed salad leaves to serve

1 Preheat the grill to high. Blanch the leeks in a pan of lightly salted boiling water for 2 minutes. Add the spring onions and spinach just before the end of the cooking time. Drain, rinse in cold water and dry on kitchen paper.

2 Whisk together the eggs, milk and nutmeg. Season with salt and pepper. Stir the goat's cheese into the egg mixture with the leeks, spinach and spring onions.

3 Heat the oil in a non-stick frying pan. Pour in the frittata mixture and fry gently for 4–5 minutes, then finish under the hot grill for 4–5 minutes, until the top is golden and just firm. Serve with mixed salad.

EASY		NUTRITIONAL INFORMATION	Serves
Preparation Time 10 minutes	**Cooking Time** 12 minutes	**Per Serving** 281 calories, 21g fat (of which 9g saturates), 3g carbohydrate, 0.9g salt	**4**

Red Onion Tarte Tatin

50g (2oz) butter

2 tbsp olive oil

1.1kg (2½lb) red onions, sliced into rounds

1 tbsp light muscovado sugar

175ml (6fl oz) white wine

4 tsp white wine vinegar

1 tbsp freshly chopped thyme, plus extra to garnish (optional)

450g (1lb) puff pastry

plain flour to dust

salt and ground black pepper

1 Lightly grease two 23cm (9in) non-stick sandwich tins with a little of the butter and set aside.

2 Melt the remaining butter with the oil in a large non-stick frying pan. Add the onions and sugar and fry for 10–15 minutes until golden, keeping the onions in their rounds.

3 Preheat the oven to 220°C (200°C fan) mark 7. Add the wine, vinegar and thyme to the pan. Bring to the boil and let it bubble until the liquid has evaporated. Season with salt and pepper, then divide the mixture between the tins and leave to cool.

4 Halve the pastry. On a lightly floured surface, roll out each piece thinly into a round shape just larger than the sandwich tin. Put one pastry round over the onion mixture in each tin and tuck in the edges. Prick the pastry dough all over with a fork.

5 Cook the tarts for 15–20 minutes until the pastry is risen and golden. Take out of the oven and put a large, warm plate over the pastry. Turn the whole thing over and shake gently to release the tart, then remove the tin. Scatter with thyme, if you like, and cut into wedges to serve.

Get Ahead

To prepare ahead Complete the recipe to the end of step 4. Cover and keep in the fridge for up to 24 hours.
To use Complete the recipe.

Serves	EASY		NUTRITIONAL INFORMATION
12	**Preparation Time** 15 minutes	**Cooking Time** 35–40 minutes	**Per Serving** 235 calories, 15g fat (of which 3g saturates), 23g carbohydrate, 0.4g salt

Cook's Tip

Yogurt Sauce
Mix 225g (8oz) Greek yogurt with 1 crushed garlic clove and 2 tbsp freshly chopped coriander. Season with salt and pepper. Chill until ready to serve.

12 baby onions

12 new potatoes

12 button mushrooms

2 courgettes

2 garlic cloves, crushed

1 tsp each ground coriander and turmeric

½ tsp ground cumin

1 tbsp sun-dried tomato paste

1 tsp chilli sauce

juice of ½ lemon

4 tbsp olive oil

275g (10oz) smoked tofu, cut into 2.5cm (1in) cubes

salt and ground black pepper

Yogurt Sauce (see Cook's Tip) and lemon wedges to serve

Spicy Vegetable Kebabs

1 Blanch the baby onions in a pan of lightly salted boiling water for 3 minutes, then drain, refresh in cold water and peel away the skins. Put the potatoes into a pan of lightly salted cold water, bring to the boil and parboil for 8 minutes, then drain and refresh under cold water. Blanch the mushrooms in boiling water for 1 minute, then drain and refresh under cold water. Cut each courgette into six chunky slices and blanch for 1 minute, then drain and refresh.

2 Mix the garlic, spices, tomato paste, chilli sauce, lemon juice, olive oil, salt and pepper together in a shallow dish. Add the well-drained vegetables and tofu and toss to coat. Cover and chill for several hours or overnight.

3 Preheat the barbecue or grill. Soak four wooden skewers in water for 20 minutes. Thread the vegetables and tofu on to the skewers. Cook the kebabs for 8–10 minutes until the vegetables are charred and tender, turning frequently and basting with the marinade. Serve with Yogurt Sauce and lemon wedges.

Serves 4	EASY		NUTRITIONAL INFORMATION	
	Preparation Time 30 minutes, plus marinating	**Cooking Time** 10 minutes plus soaking	**Per Serving** 247 calories, 14g fat (of which 3g saturates), 22g carbohydrate, 0.1g salt	Vegan Gluten free

Cook's Tips

Garam masala
Sold ready prepared, this Indian spice mix is aromatic rather than hot.

To make your own garam masala
Grind together 10 green cardamom pods, 1 tbsp black peppercorns and 2 tsp cumin seeds. Store in an airtight container and use within one month.

Tamarind paste
This has a very sharp, sour flavour and is widely used in Asian and South East Asian cooking.

Chickpea Curry

2 tbsp vegetable oil

2 onions, finely sliced

2 garlic cloves, crushed

1 tbsp ground coriander

1 tsp mild chilli powder

1 tbsp black mustard seeds

2 tbsp tamarind paste (see Cook's Tips)

2 tbsp sun-dried tomato paste

750g (1lb 10oz) new potatoes, quartered

400g can chopped tomatoes

1 litre (1¾ pints) hot vegetable stock

250g (9oz) green beans, trimmed

2 × 400g cans chickpeas, drained and rinsed

2 tsp garam masala (see Cook's Tips)

salt and ground black pepper

1 Heat the oil in a pan and fry the onions for 10–15 minutes until golden – when they have a good colour they will add depth of flavour. Add the garlic, coriander, chilli, mustard seeds, tamarind paste and sun-dried tomato paste. Cook for 1–2 minutes until the aroma from the spices is released.

2 Add the potatoes and toss in the spices for 1–2 minutes. Add the tomatoes and hot stock, season with salt and pepper, and then cover and bring to the boil. Reduce the heat and simmer, half-covered, for 20 minutes or until the potatoes are just cooked.

3 Add the beans and chickpeas and continue to cook for 5 minutes or until the beans are tender and the chickpeas are warmed through. Stir in the garam masala and serve.

EASY		NUTRITIONAL INFORMATION		Serves
Preparation Time 20 minutes	**Cooking Time** 40–45 minutes	**Per Serving** 291 calories, 8g fat (of which 1g saturates), 46g carbohydrate, 1.3g salt	Vegan	**6**

5

Sweet Treats

Try Something Different

Replace the lemon with orange, the pecans with walnut halves and the whiskey with Cointreau.

Maple Pecan Pie

250g (9oz) plain flour, sifted

a large pinch of salt

225g (8oz) unsalted butter, cubed and chilled

100g (3½oz) light muscovado sugar

125g (4oz) dates, stoned and roughly chopped

grated zest and juice of ½ lemon

100ml (3½fl oz) maple syrup, plus 6 tbsp extra

1 tsp vanilla extract

4 medium eggs

300g (11oz) pecan nut halves

300ml (½ pint) double cream

2 tbsp bourbon whiskey

1 Put the flour and salt into a food processor. Add 125g (4oz) butter and whizz to fine crumbs; add 2 tbsp water and whizz until the mixture just comes together. Wrap in clingfilm and chill for 30 minutes. Use to line a 28 × 4cm (11 × 1½in) loose-bottomed tart tin, then cover and chill for 30 minutes. Preheat the oven to 200°C (180°C fan oven) mark 6.

2 Prick the pastry all over, cover with greaseproof paper and fill with baking beans. Bake for 25 minutes, then remove the paper and beans and bake for a further 5 minutes or until the base is dry and light golden.

3 Meanwhile, whizz the rest of the butter in a food processor to soften. Add the sugar and dates and whizz to cream together. Add the lemon zest and juice, 100ml (3½fl oz) maple syrup, the vanilla extract, eggs and 200g (7oz) nuts. Whizz until the nuts are finely chopped – the mixture will look curdled. Pour into the pastry case and top with the rest of the nuts.

4 Bake for 40–45 minutes until almost set in the middle. Cover with greaseproof paper for the last 10 minutes if the nuts turn very dark. Cool slightly before removing from the tin, then brush with 4 tbsp maple syrup. Lightly whip the cream with the whiskey and 2 tbsp maple syrup, then serve with the pie.

EASY		NUTRITIONAL INFORMATION	Serves
Preparation Time 40 minutes, plus chilling	**Cooking Time** 1¼ hours	**Per Serving** 748 calories, 57g fat (of which 24g saturates), 51g carbohydrate, 0.6g salt	**10**

Cook's Tip

Slightly overripe bananas are ideal for this recipe.

Sticky Banoffee Pies

150g (5oz) digestive biscuits

75g (3oz) unsalted butter, melted, plus extra to grease

1 tsp ground ginger (optional)

450g (1lb) dulce de leche toffee sauce

4 bananas, peeled, sliced and tossed in the juice of 1 lemon

300ml (½ pint) double cream, lightly whipped

plain chocolate shavings

1 Put the biscuits into a food processor and whizz until they resemble fine crumbs. Alternatively, put them in a plastic bag and crush with a rolling pin. Transfer the biscuit mixture evenly into the bottom of 6 individual ring moulds. Divide the toffee sauce equally among the rings and top with the bananas. Pipe or spoon on the cream, sprinkle with chocolate shavings and chill. Remove from the rings or tins to serve.

Serves 6	EASY	NUTRITIONAL INFORMATION
	Preparation Time 15 minutes, plus chilling	**Per Serving** 827 calories, 55g fat (of which 32g saturates), 84g carbohydrate, 1.2g salt

Try Something Different

Use raspberries or blueberries instead of the strawberries.

Strawberry Brûlée

250g (9oz) strawberries, hulled and sliced

2 tsp golden icing sugar

1 vanilla pod

400g (14oz) Greek yogurt

100g (3½oz) golden caster sugar

1 Divide the strawberries among four ramekins and sprinkle with icing sugar.

2 Scrape the seeds from the vanilla pod and stir into the yogurt, then spread the mixture evenly over the fruit.

3 Preheat the grill to high. Sprinkle the caster sugar evenly over the yogurt until it's well covered.

4 Put the ramekins on a baking sheet or into the grill pan and grill until the sugar turns dark brown and caramelizes. Leave for 15 minutes or until the caramel is cool enough to eat, or chill for up to 2 hours before serving.

EASY		**NUTRITIONAL INFORMATION**		**Serves**
Preparation Time 15 minutes, plus chilling	**Cooking Time** 5 minutes	**Per Serving** 240 calories, 10g fat (of which 5g saturates), 35g carbohydrate, 0.2g salt	Gluten free	**4**

Cook's Tip

If you don't have any raspberry liqueur, you can use another fruit-based liqueur such as Grand Marnier instead.

Baked Raspberry Meringue Pie

8 trifle sponges

450g (1lb) raspberries, lightly crushed

2–3 tbsp raspberry liqueur

3 medium egg whites

150g (5oz) golden caster sugar

1 Preheat the oven to 230°C (210°C fan oven) mark 8. Put the trifle sponges in the bottom of a 2 litre (3½ pint) ovenproof dish. Spread the raspberries on top and drizzle with the raspberry liqueur.

2 Whisk the egg whites in a clean, grease-free bowl until stiff peaks form. Gradually whisk in the sugar until the mixture is smooth and glossy. Spoon the meringue mixture over the raspberries and bake for 6–8 minutes until golden.

Serves	EASY		NUTRITIONAL INFORMATION
8	**Preparation Time** 15 minutes	**Cooking Time** 8 minutes	**Per Serving** 176 calories, 2g fat (of which 1g saturates), 37g carbohydrate, 0.1g salt

Cook's Tips

Make double the amount of crumble topping and freeze half for an easy pudding another day.

Crumble is a great way to use leftover, slightly overripe fruit. Replace the pears with apples, or omit the blackberries and use 700g (1½lb) plums or rhubarb instead. You could also use gooseberries (omit the spice), or try 450g (1lb) rhubarb with 450g (1lb) strawberries.

Pear and Blackberry Crumble

450g (1lb) pears, peeled, cored and chopped, tossed with the juice of 1 lemon

225g (8oz) golden caster sugar

1 tsp mixed spice

450g (1lb) blackberries

cream, vanilla custard or ice cream to serve

For the crumble topping

100g (3½oz) butter, chopped, plus extra to grease

225g (8oz) plain flour

75g (3oz) ground almonds

1 Put the pears and lemon juice into a bowl, add 100g (3½oz) sugar and the mixed spice, then add the blackberries and toss thoroughly to coat.

2 Preheat the oven to 200°C (180°C fan oven) mark 6. Lightly butter a 1.8 litre (3¼ pint) shallow ovenproof dish, then carefully tip the fruit into the dish in an even layer.

3 To make the topping, put the butter, flour, ground almonds and the remaining sugar into a food processor and pulse until the mixture begins to resemble breadcrumbs. Tip into a bowl. (Alternatively, rub the butter into the flour in a large bowl by hand or using a pastry cutter. Stir in the ground almonds and the remaining sugar.) Bring parts of the mixture together with your hands to make lumps.

4 Spoon the crumble topping evenly over the fruit, then bake for 35–45 minutes until the fruit is tender and the crumble is golden and bubbling. Serve with cream, custard or ice cream.

EASY		NUTRITIONAL INFORMATION	Serves
Preparation Time 20 minutes	**Cooking Time** 35–45 minutes	**Per Serving** 525 calories, 21g fat (of which 9g saturates), 81g carbohydrate, 0.3g salt	6

Try Something Different

Although wild lingonberry sauce is used here, a spoonful of any fruit sauce or compote, such as strawberry or blueberry, will taste delicious.

For an alternative presentation, serve in tumblers, layering the rice pudding with the fruit sauce; you will need to use double the amount of fruit sauce.

Fruity Rice Pudding

125g (4oz) pudding rice
1.1 litres (2 pints) full-fat milk
1 tsp vanilla extract
3–4 tbsp caster sugar
200ml (7fl oz) whipping cream
6 tbsp wild lingonberry sauce

1 Put the rice into a pan with 600ml (1 pint) cold water and bring to the boil, then reduce the heat and simmer until the liquid has evaporated. Add the milk and bring to the boil, then reduce the heat and simmer for 45 minutes or until the rice is very soft and creamy. Leave to cool.

2 Add the vanilla extract and sugar to the rice. Lightly whip the cream and fold into the pudding. Chill for 1 hour.

3 Divide the rice mixture among six glass dishes and top with 1 tbsp lingonberry sauce.

Serves 6	EASY		NUTRITIONAL INFORMATION	
	Preparation Time 10 minutes, plus cooling and chilling	**Cooking Time** 1 hour	**Per Serving** 323 calories, 17g fat (of which 10g saturates), 36g carbohydrate, 0.2g salt	Gluten free

Get Ahead

To prepare ahead Complete the recipe, cover and chill for up to two days.

Tropical Fruit and Coconut Trifle

1 small pineapple, roughly chopped

2 bananas, thickly sliced

2 × 400g cans mango slices in syrup, drained, syrup reserved

2 passion fruit, halved

175g (6oz) plain sponge, such as Madeira cake, roughly chopped

3 tbsp dark rum (optional)

200ml (7fl oz) coconut cream

500g carton fresh custard

500g carton Greek yogurt

600ml (1 pint) double cream

6 tbsp dark muscovado sugar

1 Put the pineapple pieces into a large trifle bowl, add the banana and mango slices, and spoon the passion fruit pulp over them. Top with the chopped sponge, then pour on the rum, if using, and 6 tbsp of the reserved mango syrup.

2 Mix together the coconut cream and custard and pour the mixture over the sponge.

3 Put the Greek yogurt and cream into a bowl and whisk until thick. Spoon or pipe the mixture over the custard, then sprinkle with muscovado sugar. Cover and chill for at least 1 hour before serving.

EASY	NUTRITIONAL INFORMATION	Serves
Preparation Time 30 minutes, plus chilling	**Per Serving** 404 calories, 29g fat (of which 18g saturates), 33g carbohydrate, 0.2g salt	**16**

Try Something Different

Replace the jam with ginger conserve and use ginger ice cream instead of vanilla.

1 large sponge flan case, 25.5cm (10in) in diameter

5 tbsp orange juice

7 tbsp jam – any kind

1.5 litre tub vanilla ice cream

6 large egg whites

a pinch of cream of tartar

a pinch of salt

275g (10oz) golden caster sugar

Baked Alaska

1 Put the flan case on an ovenproof plate. Spoon the orange juice over the sponge, then spread the jam over it. Scoop the ice cream on top of the jam, then put in the freezer for at least 30 minutes.

2 Put the egg whites into a large, clean, grease-free bowl and whisk until stiff. Beat in the cream of tartar and salt. Use a large spoon to fold in the sugar, 1 tbsp at a time, then whisk until very thick and shiny.

3 Spoon the meringue over the ice cream to cover, making sure that the meringue is sealed to the flan case edge all the way round. Freeze for at least 1 hour or overnight.

4 Preheat the oven to 230°C (210°C fan oven) mark 8. Bake for 3–4 minutes until the meringue is tinged golden brown. Serve immediately. If the Baked Alaska has been in the freezer overnight, bake and leave to stand for about 15 minutes before serving.

Serves	EASY		NUTRITIONAL INFORMATION
8	**Preparation Time** 30 minutes, plus freezing	**Cooking Time** 3–4 minutes	**Per Serving** 532 calories, 16g fat (of which 9g saturates), 93g carbohydrate, 0.5g salt

Quick Gooey Chocolate Puddings

100g (3½oz) unsalted butter, plus extra to grease

100g (3½oz) golden caster sugar, plus extra to dust

100g (3½oz) plain chocolate (at least 70 per cent cocoa solids), broken into pieces

2 large eggs

20g (¾oz) plain flour

icing sugar to dust

1 Preheat the oven to 200°C (180°C fan oven) mark 6. Butter four 200ml (7fl oz) ramekins and dust with sugar. Melt the chocolate and butter in a heatproof bowl set over a pan of gently simmering water, making sure the base of the bowl doesn't touch the water. Take the bowl off the pan and leave to cool for 5 minutes.

2 Whisk the eggs, caster sugar and flour together in a bowl until smooth. Fold in the chocolate mixture and pour into the ramekins.

3 Stand the dishes on a baking tray and bake for 12–15 minutes, until the puddings are puffed and set on the outside, but still runny inside.

4 Turn out the puddings, dust with icing sugar and serve immediately.

EASY		NUTRITIONAL INFORMATION	Serves
Preparation Time 15 minutes	**Cooking Time** 12–15 minutes	**Per Serving** 468 calories, 31g fat (of which 19g saturates), 46g carbohydrate, 0.6g salt	**4**

6

Baked Bites

Sticky Lemon Polenta Cake

50g (2oz) unsalted butter, softened, plus extra to grease

3 lemons

250g (9oz) golden caster sugar

250g (9oz) instant polenta

1 tsp wheat-free baking powder

2 large eggs

50ml (2fl oz) semi skimmed milk

2 tbsp natural yogurt

2 tbsp poppy seeds

1 Preheat the oven to 180°C (160°C fan oven) mark 4. Lightly grease a 900g (2lb) loaf tin and line the base with greaseproof paper.

2 Grate the zest of 1 lemon and put into a food processor with the butter, 200g (7oz) sugar, the polenta, baking powder, eggs, milk, yogurt and poppy seeds, then whizz until smooth. Spoon the mixture into the prepared tin and level the surface. Bake for 55 minutes–1 hour until a skewer inserted into the centre comes out clean. Leave to cool in the tin for 10 minutes.

3 Next, make a syrup. Squeeze the juice from the zested lemon plus 1 more lemon. Thinly slice the third lemon. Put the lemon juice into a pan with the remaining sugar and 150ml (¼ pint) water. Add the lemon slices, bring to the boil and bubble for about 10 minutes or until syrupy. Take the pan off the heat and leave to cool for 5 minutes. Remove the lemon slices from the syrup and set aside.

4 Slide a knife around the edge of the cake and turn out on to a serving plate. Pierce the cake in several places with a skewer, spoon the syrup over it and decorate with the lemon slices.

To Store

Wrap in clingfilm and store in an airtight container. It will keep for up to three days.

Cuts into	A LITTLE EFFORT		NUTRITIONAL INFORMATION	
12	**Preparation Time** 10 minutes	**Cooking Time** 1 hour, plus cooling	**Per Slice** 220 calories, 7g fat (of which 3g saturates), 37g carbohydrate, 0.1g salt	Gluten free

To Store

Store in an airtight container. It will keep for up to five days.

Carrot Traybake

100g (3½oz) unsalted butter, chopped, plus extra to grease

140g (4½oz) carrots, grated

100g (3½oz) each sultanas and chopped dried dates

50g (2oz) tenderized coconut

1 tsp ground cinnamon and ½ tsp freshly grated nutmeg

330g bottle maple syrup

150ml (¼ pint) apple juice

zest and juice of 2 oranges

225g (8oz) wholemeal self-raising flour, sifted

2 tsp bicarbonate of soda

125g (4oz) walnut pieces

For the topping

pared zest from ½–1 orange

200g (7oz) each cream cheese and crème fraîche

2 tbsp icing sugar

1 tsp vanilla extract

1 Preheat the oven to 190°C (170°C fan oven) mark 5. Grease a 23 × 23cm (9 × 9in) cake tin and line with greaseproof paper.

2 Put the butter, carrots, sultanas, dates, coconut, spices, syrup, apple juice, and orange zest and juice into a large pan. Cover and bring to the boil, then cook for 5 minutes. Tip into a bowl and leave to cool.

3 Put the flour, bicarbonate of soda and walnuts into a large bowl and stir together. Add the cooled carrot mixture and stir well. Spoon the mixture into the prepared tin and level the surface.

4 Bake for 45 minutes–1 hour until firm. Leave to cool in the tin for 10 minutes, then turn out on to a wire rack to cool completely.

5 To make the topping, finely slice the orange zest. Put the cream cheese, crème fraîche, icing sugar and vanilla into a bowl and stir with a spatula. Spread over the cake and top with the zest. Cut into 15 squares to serve.

Cuts into 15	EASY		NUTRITIONAL INFORMATION
	Preparation Time 30 minutes	**Cooking Time** 50 minutes–1 hour 5 minutes	**Per Square** 399 calories, 25g fat (of which 13g saturates), 41g carbohydrate, 0.4g salt

To Store

Store in an airtight container. They will keep for up to one week.

Almond Macaroons

2 medium egg whites

125g (4oz) caster sugar

125g (4oz) ground almonds

¼ tsp almond extract

22 blanched almonds

1 Preheat the oven to 180°C (160°C fan oven) mark 4. Line baking trays with baking parchment. Whisk the egg whites in a clean, grease-free bowl until stiff peaks form. Gradually whisk in the caster sugar, a little at a time, until thick and glossy. Gently stir in the ground almonds and almond extract.

2 Spoon teaspoonfuls of the mixture on to the prepared baking trays, spacing them slightly apart. Press an almond into the centre of each one and bake in the oven for 12–15 minutes until just golden and firm to the touch.

3 Leave on the baking sheets for 10 minutes, then transfer to wire racks to cool completely. On cooling, these biscuits have a soft, chewy centre; they harden up after a few days.

EASY		NUTRITIONAL INFORMATION		Makes
Preparation Time 10 minutes	**Cooking Time** 12–15 minutes, plus cooling	**Per Macaroon** 71 calories, 4g fat (of which 0.3g saturates), 7g carbohydrate, 0.1g salt	Gluten free Dairy free	**22**

To Store

Wrap the cake in clingfilm and store in an airtight container. It will keep for up to five days.

150ml (¼ pint) hot black tea, made with 2 Earl Grey tea bags

200g (7oz) sultanas

75g (3oz) ready-to-eat dried figs, roughly chopped

75g (3oz) ready-to-eat dried prunes, roughly chopped

a little vegetable oil

125g (4oz) dark muscovado sugar

2 medium eggs, beaten

225g (8oz) gluten-free flour

2 tsp wheat-free baking powder

2 tsp ground mixed spice

Fruity Teacake

1 Pour the tea into a bowl and add all the dried fruit. Leave to soak for 30 minutes.

2 Preheat the oven to 190°C (170°C fan oven) mark 5. Oil a 900g (2lb) loaf tin and line the base with greaseproof paper.

3 Beat the sugar and eggs together until pale and slightly thickened. Add the flour, baking powder, mixed spice and soaked dried fruit and tea, then mix together well. Spoon the mixture into the prepared tin and level the surface.

4 Bake on the middle shelf of the oven for 45 minutes–1 hour. Leave to cool in the tin.

5 Serve sliced, with a little butter if you like.

Cuts into	EASY		NUTRITIONAL INFORMATION	
12	**Preparation Time** 20 minutes, plus soaking	**Cooking Time** 1 hour, plus cooling	**Per Slice** 185 calories, 1g fat (of which trace saturates), 42g carbohydrate, 0.1g salt	Gluten free Dairy free

To Store

Store in an airtight container. They will keep for up to one month.

Try Something Different

Cranberry, Hazelnut and Orange Biscotti
Increase the flour to 375g (13oz), omit the cocoa powder and add the grated zest of 1 orange. Replace the chocolate chips with dried cranberries and the pistachios with chopped blanched hazelnuts.

Chocolate and Pistachio Biscotti

300g (11oz) plain flour, sifted
75g (3oz) cocoa powder, sifted
1 tsp baking powder
150g (5oz) plain chocolate chips
150g (5oz) shelled pistachio nuts
a pinch of salt
75g (3oz) unsalted butter, softened
225g (8oz) granulated sugar
2 large eggs, beaten
1 tbsp icing sugar

1 Preheat the oven to 180°C (160°C fan oven) mark 4. Line a large baking sheet with baking parchment.

2 Mix the flour with the cocoa powder, baking powder, chocolate chips, pistachio nuts and salt. Using a hand-held electric whisk, beat the butter and sugar together until light and fluffy. Gradually whisk in the beaten eggs.

3 Stir the dry ingredients into the mixture until it forms a stiff dough. With floured hands, shape the dough into two slightly flattened logs, each about 30.5 × 5cm (12 × 2in). Sprinkle with icing sugar. Put the logs on to the prepared baking sheet and bake for 40–45 minutes until they are slightly firm to the touch.

4 Leave the logs on the baking sheet for 10 minutes, then cut diagonally into 15 slices, 2cm (¾in) thick. Arrange them, cut-side down, on the baking sheet and bake again for 15 minutes or until crisp. Cool on a wire rack.

EASY		NUTRITIONAL INFORMATION	Makes
Preparation Time 15 minutes	**Cooking Time** About 1 hour, plus cooling	**Per Biscuit** 152 calories, 7g fat (of which 3g saturates), 20g carbohydrate, 0.2g salt	**30**

Try Something Different

Try making these brownies without butter – believe it or not, this recipe will still work. But you'll need to eat them within an hour of taking them out of the oven – fat is what makes cakes moist and allows them to be stored.

To Store

Complete the recipe to the end of step 6, then store in an airtight tin. They will keep for up to one week. Complete the recipe to serve.

Double-chocolate Brownies

250g (9oz) butter, plus extra to grease

250g (9oz) plain chocolate (at least 50 per cent cocoa solids), broken into pieces

100g (3½oz) white chocolate, broken into pieces

4 medium eggs

175g (6oz) light muscovado sugar

1 tsp vanilla extract

75g (3oz) plain flour, sifted

¼ tsp baking powder

1 tbsp cocoa powder, sifted, plus extra to dust

100g (3½oz) pecan nuts, chopped

a pinch of salt

a little icing sugar to dust

1 Preheat the oven to 200°C (180°C fan oven) mark 6. Grease a 20.5cm (8in) square, shallow tin and line the base with baking parchment. Melt the butter and plain chocolate in a heatproof bowl set over a pan of gently simmering water, making sure the base of the bowl doesn't touch the water. Remove the bowl from the pan and put to one side.

2 In a separate bowl, melt the white chocolate over a pan of gently simmering water, making sure the base of the bowl doesn't touch the water. Remove the bowl from the pan and put to one side.

3 Put the eggs into a separate large bowl. Add the muscovado sugar and vanilla extract and whisk together until the mixture is pale and thick.

4 Add the flour, baking powder, cocoa powder, the pecan nuts and a pinch of salt to the bowl, then carefully pour in the dark chocolate mixture. Using a large metal spoon, gently fold the ingredients together to make a smooth batter – if you fold too roughly, the chocolate will seize up and become unusable.

5 Pour the brownie mixture into the prepared tin. Spoon dollops of the white chocolate over the brownie mix, then swirl a skewer through it several times to create a marbled effect.

6 Bake for 20–25 minutes. The brownie slab should be fudgy inside and the top should be cracked and crispy. Leave to cool in the tin.

7 Transfer the slab to a board and cut into 16 individual brownies. To serve, dust with a little icing sugar and cocoa powder.

EASY		NUTRITIONAL INFORMATION	Cuts into
Preparation Time 15 minutes	**Cooking Time** 20–25 minutes, plus cooling	**Per Brownie** 352 calories, 25g fat (of which 13g saturates), 29g carbohydrate, 0.3g salt	**16**

Cook's Tip

Use dried polenta grains for this recipe.

oil to grease

125g (4oz) plain flour

175g (6oz) polenta (see Cook's Tip) or cornmeal

1 tbsp baking powder

1 tbsp caster sugar

½ tsp salt

300ml (½ pint) buttermilk, or equal quantities of natural yogurt and milk, mixed together

2 medium eggs

4 tbsp extra virgin olive oil

Corn Bread

1 Preheat the oven to 200°C (180°C fan oven) mark 6. Generously grease a 20.5cm (8in) square, shallow tin.

2 Put the flour into a large bowl, then add the polenta or cornmeal, the baking powder, sugar and salt. Make a well in the centre and pour in the buttermilk or yogurt and milk mixture. Add the eggs and olive oil and stir together until evenly mixed.

3 Pour into the tin and bake for 25–30 minutes until firm to the touch. Insert a skewer into the centre – if it comes out clean, the corn bread is done.

4 Leave the corn bread to rest in the tin for 5 minutes, then turn out and cut into chunky triangles. Serve warm with butter.

Serves	EASY		NUTRITIONAL INFORMATION
8	**Preparation Time** 5 minutes	**Cooking Time** 25–30 minutes	**Per Serving** 229 calories, 8g fat (of which 1g saturates), 33g carbohydrate, 1.3g salt

Griddled Garlic Bread

1 large crusty loaf
175g (6oz) butter, cubed
3 garlic cloves, crushed
a bunch of stiff-stemmed fresh thyme sprigs
salt and ground black pepper

1 Cut the bread into slices 2cm (¾in) thick.

2 Put the butter and garlic into a small metal or heatproof dish (a tin mug is ideal) and sit it on the barbecue grill. Leave to melt. Season with salt and pepper.

3 Dip the thyme into the melted butter and brush one side of each slice of bread. Put the slices, buttered side down, on the barbecue grill. Cook for 1–2 minutes until crisp and golden. Brush the uppermost sides with the remaining butter, turn over and cook the other side. Serve immediately.

EASY		NUTRITIONAL INFORMATION		Serves
Preparation Time 5 minutes	**Cooking Time** 5–6 minutes	**Per Serving** 400 calories, 20g fat (of which 11g saturates), 50g carbohydrate, 1.6g salt	Dairy free	**8**

Black Olive Bread

2 tsp traditional dried yeast

500g (1lb 2oz) strong white bread flour, plus extra to dust

2 tsp coarse salt, plus extra to sprinkle

6 tbsp extra virgin olive oil, plus extra to grease

100g (3½oz) black olives, pitted and chopped

1 Put 150ml (¼ pint) hand-hot water into a jug, stir in the yeast and leave for 10 minutes or until foamy. Put the flour into a bowl or a food processor, then add the salt, yeast mix, 200ml (7fl oz) warm water and 2 tbsp olive oil. Mix, using a wooden spoon or the dough hook, for 2–3 minutes to make a soft, smooth dough. Put the dough into a lightly oiled bowl, cover with oiled clingfilm and leave in a warm place for 45 minutes or until doubled in size. Punch the dough to knock out the air, then knead on a lightly floured worksurface for 1 minute. Add the olives and knead until combined. Divide in half, shape into rectangles and put into two greased tins, each about 25.5 x 15cm (10 x 6in). Cover with clingfilm and leave in a warm place for 1 hour or until the dough is puffy.

2 Preheat the oven to 200°C (180°C fan oven) mark 6. Make 12 indentations in the dough with your finger, drizzle 2 tbsp oil over the surface and sprinkle with salt. Bake for 30–35 minutes until golden. Drizzle with the remaining oil. Slice and serve warm.

Makes 2 loaves	EASY		NUTRITIONAL INFORMATION	
	Preparation Time 40 minutes, plus rising	**Cooking Time** 30–35 minutes	**Per Loaf** 600 calories, 21g fat (of which 3g saturates), 97g carbohydrate, 3.8g salt	Vegan Dairy free

Index

Collect the Easy To Makes!...

Good Housekeeping
Slow Cook
easy to make!

Good Housekeeping
Speedy Meals
easy to make!

Good Housekeeping
Chocolate
easy to make!

Good Housekeeping
Chicken
easy to make!

Good Housekeeping
Low GI
easy to make!

Good Housekeeping
Healthy Meals in Minutes
easy to make!

Good Housekeeping
Pies, Pies, Pies
easy to make!

Good Housekeeping
Cakes & Bakes
easy to make!

Good Housekeeping
Soups
easy to make!

Good Housekeeping
Family Meals in Minutes
easy to make!

Good Housekeeping
Wok & Stir-fry
easy to make!

Good Housekeeping
One Pot
easy to make!

Good Housekeeping
Puddings & Desserts
easy to make!

Good Housekeeping
Roasts
easy to make!

Good Housekeeping
Salads & Dressings
easy to make!

Good Housekeeping
Everyday Family Meals
easy to make!

Good Housekeeping
Meat Free
easy to make!

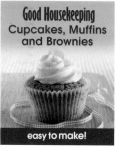
Good Housekeeping
Cupcakes, Muffins and Brownies
easy to make!

Good Housekeeping
BBQ & Grills
easy to make!

Good Housekeeping
Christmas
easy to make!

Good Housekeeping
Pasta & Noodles
easy to make!

Good Housekeeping
Curries & Spicy Meals
easy to make!

Good Housekeeping
Everyday Vegetarian
easy to make!

Good Housekeeping
Rice & Risottos
easy to make!

Good Housekeeping Institute
TRIED ★ TESTED ★ TRUSTED